PEARLS FROM THE FLOOD

Select Insight of of Shaykh al-Islam Ibrāhīm Niasse

Compiled and Translated by Zachary Wright

First published in 2015 by

Fayda Books, Publishing & Distribution
3695F Cascade Rd.
Atlanta, GA 30331

http://www.faydabooks.com
Email: orders@faydabooks.com

ISBN 978-0-9913813-9-5

Cover Design
MUHAMMADAN PRESS

Printed and bound in the United States

Thanks to Imam Cheikh Tidiane Cisse for the permission to translate, publish and print all works pertaining to Islam, Tariqa Tijaniyya and Fayda.

Pearls from the Flood

Select Insight of Shaykh al-Islam Ibrahimm Niasse

Written & Compiled by

ZACHARY WRIGHT

FAYDA
BOOKS

Contents

Acknowledgements

Gratitude from the beginning to the end is due to God.

I thank the Imam of the community of Shaykh Ibrāhīm Niasse, Shaykh al-Tijānī ʿAli Cissé, for reviewing this book and for his blessing and continued guidance. Special thanks are also due to Shaykh Ḥasan Cissé, who first gave permission for this collection in 2006. My appreciation is also due to Shaykh al-Māḥī Cissé. Such scholars, the living exemplars of the textual legacy presented here, make this translation both possible and urgently necessary. They bring Shaykh Ibrāhīm's teachings alive, so that his words become lived practice rather than relics of a bygone age.

Thanks as well to Adam Larson, Mohammad Isa, and Yahya Weldon for their editorial assistance. I thank Rudolph Ware for his continued encouragement in making the writings of West African Muslim scholars available in translation. I also appreciate the work of Ibrahim Dimson and Fayda Books in steering this work to publication.

Recognition is due to the exemplary efforts of my elders in the American Muslim community who have exerted so much effort long before me to make the writings of Shaykh Ibrāhīm available in English. I cannot hope to honor all of them by name, but certainly Shaykh Abdul-Hakim Halim, Dr. Dawud Jeffries, and Imam Sayyid Abdussalam have been inspirations for their work in this field.

All good in this book is from God, all mistakes are my own.

Imam Cheikh Tidiane Ali Cisse
Imam de la Grande Mosquée
de Médina Baye Kaolack Sénégal

الإمام الشيخ التجاني علي سيس
إمام المسجد الجامع بمدينة كولخ سنغال

هذا تقريظ للكتاب المبارك الميمون
" جـواهـر الـفيضة "

الحمد لله حمد الذات للذات والصلاة والسلام على مظهره في جميع التجليات سيدنا محمد مدد الكائنات وخاتم الرسالات وعلى ءاله وأصحابه ينابيع العلوم والخيرات والبركات ورضي الله عن خاتم الولاية المحمدية المخصوص بالختمية والكتمية وعن خليفته ووارث سره على الاطلاق دون نزاع أو شقاق سيدنا أبي إسحاق الشيخ إبراهيم انياس بن الحاج عبد الله رضى الله عنه

وبعـــد،

فان الله تبارك وتعالى ساقني بمشيئته لكى أكون من ضمن الذين وقفوا على هذا الكتاب الجليل جواهر الفيضة وهو كتاب له من الفضل ماله وله من الخير والمنفعة ماله فقد فرحت به وسررت به غاية ونهاية لما حوى من العلوم التى تنفع أهل الفيضة خاصة وكل من أراد الله نفعه من العباد فجزى الله كاتبه ومؤلفه خيرا وواصل أمداد الشيخ فيه سرا وجهرا فهو أخ خيّر وفاضل وعالم الا وهو الاستاذ الجليل والعالم النبيل السيد زكرياء رايت كثر الله خيره وزاد فى حسه ومعناه وبلغه فى الدارين متمناه فله من عندنا الرضى التامّ والمحبة الكاملة ولن أنسى ابدا ماقام وما يقوم به دائما وأسال الله متوسلا بحضرتي النبوة والولاية أن ينصره ويؤيده ويرضي عنه وعن جميع خدماته وأعماله الظاهرة والباطنه وءاخر دعوانا أن الحمد لله رب العالمين وسلام.

وكـتب الشيخ التجــاني علي سـيس
نـز يـل أكرا غـانـا
6 من جمادي الاخيرة 1436 اهـــــ

شيخ تيجان علي سيس

موبايل : ٢٢١٧٧٦٣١٧٦٤٤
فاكس : ٢٢١٣٣٩٤١٤٤٦١
صندوق بريد ٤٠٨ كولخ سنغال
الإيميل:

Tél: 221 77 ... 26 ...
Fax: 221 ... 41 44 61
BP: 408 KAOLACK SENEGAL
Email: ...@msn.com
... cheikh...@yahoo.fr

Imam Cheikh Tidiane Aly CISSE Imam de la Grande Mosquée de Médina Baye Kaolack Sénégal
الإمام الشيخ التجاني علي سيس إمام المسجد الجامع بمدينة كولخ

Commendation for the blessed and auspicious book

Pearls from the Flood

By Shaykh al-Tijānī Cissé

[Abridged translation]

All praise to Allāh, praise of the Essence, belonging to the Essence. Blessing and peace on His manifestation among the entirety of manifestations, our master Muḥammad, the support of the created entities, the seal of messengers; and upon his family and companions following after in knowledge, virtue, and blessing. May Allāh be pleased with the seal of Muḥammadan sainthood, uniquely distinguished to be the seal, and to be hidden. And (may He be pleased) with his successor, the unlimited inheritor of his secret, without dispute or dissension, our master Abī Isḥāq al-Shaykh Ibrāhīm Niasse b. al-Ḥājj ʿAbd-Allāh.

Allāh the Most High and Exalted has directed me by His will to be among the guarantors for whoever should come upon this distinguished book, *Pearls of the Flood*. This book contains grace, goodness, and benefit. It has brought me happiness and satisfaction from the beginning to the end for what it contains of knowledge for the people of the Divine Flood especially, and for whomever Allāh desires benefit among His servants. So may Allāh reward its writer and compiler with goodness, and may the support of the Shaykh continue to be with him, secretly and openly, for he is a brother endowed with grace, virtue, and knowledge: the distinguished professor and noble scholar, *al-Sayyid* Zakariya Wright […]

And our final prayer is to praise Allāh, Lord of all the worlds. Peace.

Shaykh al-Tijānī b. ʿAlī Cissé
Imam of the Grand Mosque
Medina-Baye Kaolack, Senegal

Accra, Ghana
March 26, 2015

Translator's Introduction

This book gathers some of the key discourses of the renowned Senegalese "Shaykh al-Islām" Ibrāhīm b. ʿAbd-Allāh Niasse (d. 1975). Shaykh Ibrāhīm was undoubtedly one of the twentieth century's most renowned Muslim intellectuals. Indeed, he engaged with a variety of questions pertaining to contemporary Muslim identities: changes in Islamic learning, spiritual training, anti-colonial liberation, or the politics of community building, for example. *Pearls from the Flood* translates a wide range of primary source material that speaks to the Shaykh's spectrum of intellectual and social roles. These sources should be read in the context of Shaykh Ibrāhīm's historical positioning within relevant Muslim and African discourses. This introduction thus provides a short overview of the Shaykh's intellectual biography relating to Sufism, Islamic learning more generally, African decolonization, and post-colonial visions of Islamic solidarity.

As a leading scholar of the Tijāniyya Sufi order in modern times, Shaykh Ibrāhīm was the spiritual guide to millions of Sufi aspirants throughout Africa and beyond. His followers knew him as the paradigmatic inheritor (*khalīfa*) of the "Seal of Saints" Shaykh A*h*mad al-Tijānī (d. 1815, Fez), and thus the axial saint (*quṭb*) of his age. Shaykh Ibrāhīm's community distinguished itself historically by an unprecedented transmission of the experiential knowledge (*ma'rifa*) of God. This was based on the Shaykh's claim to possess the "flood" (*fayḍa*), an overflowing divine grace (*faḍl*) reconnecting the Muslim community to God in an age of corruption.

I said: "There is no god but Allāh,

and Muḥammad has been sent by Allāh."

Then from me overflowed His secret, and whoever seeks me with purpose

Attains the knowledge of Allāh, the Eternal Sustainer

The elders the same as the youth

Since the Beloved, the Sanctuary has come close

The men the same as the women

The poor the same as the sultans.

Shaykh Ibrāhīm's words, here from the poem "The Bursting Flood" included in this collection, thus communicate a sense of urgency: humanity, and Muslims especially, must strive for the cognizance or gnosis (*ma'rifa*) of God. Such knowledge is the essential purpose of human existence.

If the Shaykh's endowment with *fayḍa* offered his students direct access to *ma'rifa*, he also demonstrated recognizable mastery of other doctrines and practices long held dear to the Sufi tradition. His writings and speeches are thus filled with references to the remembrance (*dhikr*) of God, purification of the self (*tazkiyat al-nafs*), love of the Prophet, friendship (*walāya*) with God, and comportment on the spiritual path (*adab al-*

sulūk). The actual practice of Sufism is of course inseparable from apprenticeship to a guiding master (*shaykh al-murshid*). According to noted Islamicist William Chittick, "All Sufis agree that entering the path without a shaykh is impossible. If someone thinks he has done so, in fact he has gone astray."[1] Shaykh Ibrāhīm explained the disciple's special relationship to the spiritual guide by citing the words of Abū Madyan:

> *The shaykh is someone whom your subjective being (dhāt) has acknowledged with preference, and whom your innermost being (sirr) has acknowledged with reverence. The shaykh refines you with his exemplary character, trains (addaba) you by bowing his head in silence, and illuminates your inner being with his radiance. The shaykh is he who gathers you in his presence and preserves you in his absence.*[2]

Accented here is the gentle beauty of "love for the sake of God" within the shaykh-disciple relationship, so often lost in academic discussion of the practice. Indeed, the sacred bond between the shaykh and the disciple cannot be reduced to words. But the ineffability of such core doctrines and practices of course did not stop Sufi intellectuals from producing a rich corpus of writing. While the current collection does not present a comprehensive overview of the Shaykh's Sufi thought, it demonstrates his familiar access to Sufism's deep knowledge tradition.

Shaykh Ibrāhīm's writing and speeches readily display mastery of the Islamic knowledge disciplines (ʿulūm al-dīn) more broadly. Particilarly discernable is his knowledge of Arabic grammar (*naḥw*), literature (*adab*), theology (ʿaqīda), juris-

---

1 William Chittick, *The Sufi Path of Knowledge: Ibn al-ʿArabi's Metaphysics of Imagination* (Albany: SUNY Press, 1989), 270.

2 Abū Madyan (d. 1198, Tlemcen) cited in Niasse, *Kāshif al-ilbās ʿan fayḍat al-khatm Abī l-ʿAbbās* (Cairo: al-sharika al-dawliyya, 2001), 136.

prudence (*fiqh*), Prophetic traditions (*ḥadīth*), and Qurʾān exegesis (*tafsīr*). The Shaykh learned these sciences at an early age, mostly in the distinguished learning circle (*majlis al-ʿilm*) of his father, al-Ḥājj ʿAbd-Allāh b. Muḥammad Niasse (d. 1922). Al-Ḥājj ʿAbd-Allāh had attracted students from all over Senegal and Mauritania. On the way to Mecca to accomplish the pilgrimage, his erudition so impressed the scholars of Egypt's Azhar University that they conferred on him an honorary diploma.[3] Aside from his father's authorization to teach, Shaykh Ibrāhīm's collection of scholarly licences (*ijāzāt*) in the religious sciences include unlimited authorizations from some of the most renowned traditional scholars in the Muslim world: ʿAbd al-Ḥayy al-Kattānī of Morocco, ʿAbd-Allāh b. al-Ṭayyib al-Azharī of Egypt, Ṣāliḥ b. al-Fuḍayl al-Tūnisī of Medina Arabia, Aḥmad Sukayrij of Morocco, and Muḥammad al-Ḥāfiẓ al-Tijānī of Egypt.[4] Several learned students of Shaykh Ibrāhīm, chief among them the Shaykh's successor (*khalīfa*) Sayyid ʿAlī b. al-Ḥasan Cissé, thus obtained from him a comprehensive authorization through multiple illustrious chains of transmission (*asānīd*; sing: *sanad*). Indeed, at least by the early 1960s, Shaykh Ibrāhīm had become known, in Arab world press reports and elsewhere, as the "Shaykh al-Islām" or simply the "Leader" (*zaʿīm*), of Muslims in West Africa.

Lead by such an African "Shaykh al-Islām" at the moment of decolonization, Shaykh Ibrāhīm's community has maintained a certain anti-colonial and pan-African and pan-Islamic stance. Internal discourses remember a three-decade campaign, beginning in the 1930s, of spiritual Jihād against colonial occupation employing the weaponry of self-reliance

3 Ibrahim Niang, "Āthār al-taṣawwuf fī ḥayāt al-Ḥājj ʿAbd-Allāh Inīyās" (Conference paper: *Semaine al-Hajj Abdoulaye Niasse*, Dakar, 1986). Copy in author's possession.

4 For more discussion of Niasse's *Majmūʿ al-ijāzāt*, see Zachary Wright, *Living Knowledge in West African Islam: the Sufi Community of Ibrāhīm Niasse* (Leiden: Brill, 2015), 194-197.

and prayer.[5] The community's distance from colonial power and its rapid spread after the Second World War unnerved British and French colonial authorities. The Shaykh's surveillance file in the colonial archives is probably the largest of any African scholar. In 1955, one colonial official warned that with Niasse's growing following "there is a risk of seeing the impending creation of a State for the black race with a Muslim political and social structure."[6]

Indeed, Shaykh Ibrāhīm's millions of followers mostly spread between Mauritania, Nigeria, and Sudan, constituted arguably the most successful Afro-Islamic revivalist movement of modern times. Such an international network occasioned significant reflection on the nature of post-colonial solidarities beyond the narrowly defined nation-state. Shaykh Ibrāhīm became friends with pan-Africanist anti-colonial intellectuals like Kwame Nkrumah of Ghana and Ahmad Sekou Touré of Gineau. He campaigned in travels, speeches, and writings for the ideals of pan-African solidarity, encouraging all Africans to "liberate themselves and raise the pan-African banner, so that they may practice their beliefs and traditions freely."[7] He told a large gathering in Nigeria: "I believe it is incumbent on all the African nations to one day unify, in order to facilitate cooperation between themselves: a cooperation that will be quite fruitful."[8]

---

5 See Wright, *Living Knowledge*, 255-258.

6 Sous-Directeur Bougeau, 4 June 1955; cited in Rüdiger Seesemann, "Nach der Flut: Ibrahim Niasse Sufik Und Gesellschaft in Westafrika" (PhD Dissertation, University of Bayreuth, 2004), 868.

7 Ibrāhīm Niasse to Ahmad Bello, March 1961; cited in Jonathan Reynolds, *The Time of Politics (Zaminin Siyasa): Islam and the Politics of Legitimacy in Northern Nigeria 1950–1966* (Bethesda, MD: International Scholars Publications, 1999), 194.

8 Ibrāhīm Niasse, *Jawāhir al-rasā'il* (Nigeria: Aḥmad Abū l-Fatḥ, unknown date), II:132–133.

Significantly, the Shaykh did not see confessional differences as an impediment to mutual cooperation for common goals. In 1961, he told an international gathering in Ghana, whose audience included Kwame Nkrumah, Josip Tito of Yugoslavia, and Leonid Breshnev of the Soviet Union:

> *I see the world as one great village that the people of different religions share. And in this village, whatever their confessional differences, the inhabitants can unite under the tree to discuss during the day, to reflect on what might undermine or bring favor to their hopes. However, as soon as each person is in the enclosure of his hut, nobody can prohibit him from exercising his religion. I am sure every parent will have an idea as to how to best guide their own children.*[9]

Shaykh Ibrāhīm of course encouraged the involvement of righteous Muslims in politics, but he shied from supporting any specifically Muslim political agenda. Within Senegal, he cultivated a distant cooperation with the country's founding president, a Christian, Leopold Senghor. The Shaykh seemed to define politics simply as "providing benefit to people." Muslim politicians, like any other politicians, must be challenged to help people: that is what defined their worth, not their religious affiliation.

> *The creation is the family of God, and the most beloved to Him are those who provide for His family ... "God helps the servant as long as the servant is helping his brother." With these attributes, we become the best of communities brought forth for mankind.*[10]

---

9 Niasse's words according to Barham Diop, interview, Dakar, August 2006, and September 2011. The same speech is cited in Mouhamadou Mahdy Niasse, *Baye Niass: Le Défenseur de l'Islam* (Montreal: Alioune Thiam, 1997), 50. The last sentence, however, was provided only in Diop's September 2011 interview.

10 Ibrāhīm Niasse, *Jawāhir al-rasā'il*, II: 9.

Such an emphasis on justice essentially defined the Shaykh's political engagement. He was thus fond of reciting the Islamic adage: "A believer can live for a long time with those of no faith, but he will not last long with the unjust."[11]

Beyond the ideals of pan-African cooperation during decolonization, Shaykh Ibrāhīm's community articulated its own vision of global Islamic solidarity. Unlike other modern Islamic movements, this vision explicitly denounced what may sometimes appear as the thinly veiled ethno-centrism of reformist calls (such as Arab socialism, the Muslim Brotherhood, or Salafism) emerging from the Arab world.

> *The truth is that, for the last three centuries, you have not seen anyone who has raised up the religion in history—either by knowledge, guidance, or struggle (jihād)—except that he was a non-Arab. This proves the statement of the one who said: "Islam will remain with the Arabs, but it will be strengthened by the non-Arabs." The non-Arabs, they are those who strengthen Islam. There are seven hundred million Muslims today, and the Arabs pride themselves that they make up one hundred million ... Whether among Arabs or non-Arabs, Islam entails holding fast to this religion and not turning to nationalisms (qawmiyyāt), racialisms (ʿunṣuriyyāt), and pagan ignorance (jāhiliyya). The most honored of you in the presence of God is the most pious.*[12]

In a Muslim world increasingly racialized by the experience of colonialism, Muslims needed to rethink their common association of the Arab race with Islamic orthodoxy. The community

11 Ibrāhīm Niasse, "Eternal Islam," see selection later in this volume. The Shaykh echoed a similar sentiment in a 1971 speech in Kaduna, Nigeria. See Niasse, *Saʿādat al-anām bi aqwāl shaykh al-islām* (Cairo: al-sharika al-dawliyya, 2006), 33.

12 Ibrāhīm Niasse, "Khuṭbat ḥadīqat al-anwār" (in Kano, Nigeria, 1960s), in *Saʿādat al-anām*, 118–119. The final quotation is from the Qurʾān.

thus created ideological space for a global revivalist network whose heart remained in black Africa.

Shaykh Ibrāhīm also avoided the common reformist manipulation of the Islamic traditional sciences that tends to direct virulent attacks against the variety of opinions in the legal schools (*madhāhib*) or the methods of spiritual purification in the Sufi orders (*ṭuruq*). According to such reformist discourses, the defeat of the Muslim world can be blamed on superstitious accretions (allegedly Sufism) and the practice of following scholars instead of sacred texts. Shaykh Ibrāhīm openly castigated such associations, and suggested that the problem was actually the turning away from the exemplars of the Islamic cultural order.

> *When the enemies of Islam wanted to forcibly tear apart Islam, they began by driving people away from the friends of God (awliyāʾ). When they finished with that, they alienated people from the ritual prayer. Then they alienated them from the religion completely. Thus, we hear many in this time who disavow the Tijāniyya Sufi order.*[13]

Shaykh Ibrāhīm's vision of global Islamic solidarity thus depended on the Muslim community's recognition of Islamic exemplars, or "friends of God," whose very being-in-the-world inspired meaning and purpose to contemporary Muslim identities.

But the question of community solidarities may exaggerate certain contextualized responses to immediate concerns. Most of Shaykh Ibrāhīm's public statements downplayed sectarian divides and asserted the sacred unity of the Muslim world. In practice, he met with various Saudi kings and scholars, was photographed with Mawlana Mawdudi of the Pakistani Jamaat-e Islami, and wrote Egyptian president Gamal Abdel

13 Niasse, "Khuṭbat ḥadīqat al-anwār," in *Saʿādat al-anām*, 117.

Nasser to stop the execution of Muslim Brotherhood intellectual Sayyid Qutb.[14]

Perhaps the only feature that has consistently united Shaykh Ibrāhīm's vast and diverse network of followers as a distinctive community has been an uncompromising desire for the direct knowledge (*maʿrifa*) of God. The understanding of Shaykh Ibrāhīm's popularity cannot overstate the appeal of *maʿrifa*. Here is the Shaykh's explanation of the divine "attraction" (*jadhb*) through which aspirants obtain *maʿrifa*, here taken from his primary work on Sufism, the *Kāshif al-ilbās*:

> *Know that when a servant comes near to God through supererogatory good works, God enraptures (yajdhabu) him, loving him with a forceful attraction (jadhban). In this (rapture), the servant is not aware of himself, or anything else; neither what came before nor what will come after, neither of any part of himself, nor the whole of himself. He becomes absent from his personal witnessing (shuhūd), and is consumed in the intensity of his Master's summoning, glorious and exalted is He. In this state, he witnesses the divine presence (ḥaḍra), as before the world and after the hereafter, as before the before and after the after. This presence has no beginning and no end, no above and no below, no right and no left, no explanation (kayf) and no definition, no name and no attribute, no going forward and no going back, no connection and no separation, no going in and no going out, no sensation and no realization (idrāk), no incarnation (ḥulūl) and no fusion (ittiḥād). The lover becomes extinct in his Beloved. And he becomes extinct to his own extinction (fanāʾ). Nothing remains except the divine selfhood (al-Huwiyya).*[15]

14 Wright, *Living Knowledge*, 277-280.
15 Ibrāhīm Niasse, *Kāshif al-ilbās*, 147–148.

As previously mentioned, this experiential knowledge of God was the essential purpose for which humanity was created. The Shaykh wrote in his first poem, *Rūḥ al-adab*: "Whoever does not obtain knowledge of the Merciful [God], his life has been in ruin for all time spent." [16]

Pearls from the Flood provides primary source material for the ongoing study of Sufism in the contemporary world, and especially for the understanding of Shaykh Ibrāhīm's "Community of the Flood" (*jamāʿat al-fayḍa*). From the perspective of traditional learning, the availability of such source material does not obviate the need for living teachers. From an academic perspective, source translations do not take the place of scholarly analysis. In my own research on the community of Ibrāhīm Niasse, I have made a case for understanding Muslim religious identities on their own terms. Reliable translations therefore become imperative. This work hopes to illuminate Shaykh Ibrāhīm's broad scholarly corpus, adding to the earlier translation of his primary work on Sufism, the *Kāshif al-ilbās* (Fons Vitae, 2010) and the translation of his Qurʾān exegesis, *Fī riyāḍ al-tafsīr* (Fayda Books, 2014). As illustrative excerpts from Shaykh Ibrāhīm's voluminous speeches, letters, poetry, and supplications, this book offers little more than a surface sampling. Nonetheless, I attempted to identify some of the key tracts, letters, and verses that Shaykh Ibrāhīm's followers reference to the present day.

An earlier rendition of this book was attempted with *Pearls from the Divine Flood: Selected Discourses of Shaykh Ibrahim Niasse* (African American Islamic Institute, 2006). Roughly half of that book (in revised form) makes its way into this book. Significantly, this includes a reprint of Shaykh Ḥasan Cissé's formative overview of his grandfather Shaykh Ibrāhīm's

16 Ibrāhīm Niasse, *Rūḥ al-adab*, in Ḥasan Cissé, *Spirit of Good Morals by Shaykh al-Islam Ibrahim Niasse, Translation and Commentary* (Detroit: African American Islamic Institute, 2001), 70.

life and legacy first written in 1984 (see appendix). Stylistically, the reader will be aware that I have sometimes used alternate translations for the same word, especially where the Arabic word has proven notoriously difficult to approximate with one English equivalent. For example, *maʿrifa* becomes "gnosis", "cognizance", or just "knowledge" depending on the context. *Taqwā* appears alternatively as "fear", "awe", or "piety." In most cases, I have inserted the translitered Arabic word in parenthesis for more precise reading. This translation adopts the normative transliteration format used by most academic publishers in English. I have sometimes omitted the customary magnifications of God and salutations on the Prophet Muḥammad found in Islamic religious texts, but mostly these formalities are translated in the text where they could be integrated into the sentence structure.

The intention in publishing this book is to make available some of the key sources that have informed my own research on the community of Shaykh Ibrāhīm Niasse. I originally thought to include this material as an appendix to the more academic publication, *Living Knowledge in West African Islam* (Brill, 2015). However, *Pearls from the Flood* is an attempt to honor the rights of a public, non-Arabic speaking audience desiring more direct access to these sources. I hope that English readers can find benefit from Shaykh Ibrāhīm's words in this book.

Chapter I

Public Discourses in Arabic

Reflections on the Human Condition

Shaykh Ibrāhīm gave the following address in Cairo in 1961.[17] The venue was the chief *zāwiya* of the Tijāniyya in Egypt, established by the renowned Shaykh Muḥammad al-Ḥāfiẓ (d. 1979).

* * *

My distinguished brothers: Peace to you and the mercy and blessing of Allāh the Most High. I am happy to be in this house, especially in this blessed evening and in this night, and I praise Allāh, who by His beautiful veil, you see in me your own good and beautiful attributes, and it is not I who possess them. As has been said in verse:

They think good of me, and there is no good in me

But I am as offensive a slave as can be imagined

Glory to You my Lord! All of my defects have been hidden from their eyes

A complete grace from You, the gift of Your veil.

17 The Arabic version of address is found in Niasse, *Jawāhir al-rasāʾil*, II: 3-7.

Indeed, you have seen your own beautiful qualities, and they are nothing but the veil of Allāh, the Beautiful. I praise Allāh for this, and I commend you for the excellence of your thoughts. As it has come to us: "There are two traits that nothing exceeds: to think well of Allāh and to think well of Allāh's servants." I came to you as an ordinary visitor, not with the attribute of leadership (but you have nonetheless accorded me the reception worthy of a leader). You have thus confirmed the words (of the Prophet), "Each one of you is a shepherd, and each shepherd is responsible for his flock."[18] Being that each of us is a shepherd, each of us is then a leader (*zaʿīm*).

And as for myself, I am a model for nothing except that I love Islam, and I love my Muslim brothers wherever they are. This love is surely an important matter before Allāh, as all the religious scholars have indicated. And this is because a man is with whom he loves, and he who loves a people gathers with them. "Two people who love each other for the sake of Allāh will be under His shade on a day when there will be no shade except His shade."[19]

I bear witness to you that I love all of you for the sake of Allāh, as I witness that you love me for the sake of Allāh. This is my hope for myself and you, as a man is many with his brother. The truth is that our religion is a religion of congregation in pursuit of all of the good things of this world and the next, and it is a religion of unity. The religion of Islam is a religion of struggle (*kafāh*), (but also) a religion of brotherhood, a religion of freedom, a religion of equality. Allāh has indicated this in His Book, which is the constitution for every time and place. As for the constitutions the orators are pointing to, all of these constitutions are deficient, limited by a particular time. The

18 Ḥadīth on the authority of Ibn ʿUmar, related by Bukhārī and Muslim; included in *Riyāḍ al-Ṣāliḥīn*, chapter 35, no. 285.

19 Variations of this Ḥadīth, on the authority of Abu Hurayra, are related by Muslim and Bukhārī; included in *Riyāḍ al-Ṣāliḥīn*, chapter 46, no. 379-380.

Qur'ān is the lasting and inclusive constitution for the entire world. "We have left out nothing in the Book."[20]

Islam is a religion of unity, by His exalted word: "*And hold fast, all together, to the rope of Allāh, and do not separate.*"[21] And it is a religion of submission: "*And Allāh is calling to an abode of peace.*"[22] The Prophet said to the mighty ones of the land, "Submit! You will be safe, and Allāh will give you double reward." Indeed, Islam is based on peace: "A Muslim is he who safeguards the Muslims from his tongue and his hand." So if this is the religion, it is a religion of peace. And it is a religion of equality: "There is no preference for an Arab over a non-Arab except by piety (*taqwā*)."[23]

We, then, love you for the sake of Allāh, and you love us for the sake of Allāh. And (what can) I say (after this except) that I am advising myself and you with the awe (*taqwā*) of Allāh in secret and public, and with the observation of Him with every breath. If the servant of Allāh strives with these two traits, he will gain two praiseworthy attributes. *Taqwā* is the obedience to His command, as well as the avoiding of abomination externally and internally. The external *taqwā* entails taking account of the limbs of the body. The hidden *taqwā* entails taking account of the hidden and the secret.

We hear from many of the saints and from our Shaykh Tijānī about the working of miracles, and we also hear about miracles from the scholars. But they have done nothing except possess these two traits: the awe of Allāh and observation of Him. If each of us feared Allāh and observed Him with each of his breaths, nothing would remain with him except Allāh.

---

20 Qur'ān, 6:38.

21 Qur'ān, 3:103.

22 Qur'ān, 10:25.

23 Words of the Prophet Muḥammad from his last sermon, related by nearly every Ḥadīth collection (Bukhārī, Muslim, Tirmidhī, etc.).

"*And Allāh is victorious over his affair,*"[24] and nothing incapacitates Him in the earth or in heaven.[25] If you are created with these two traits, they are the warrantors of all that is loved in this world and the next.

And (as for) mankind, Allāh has said in His mighty book: "*And when your Lord said to the angels, I am placing on the earth a representative* (*khalīfa*)." This was Adam, father of humanity. The angels said, "'*Will you place (on the earth) one who spreads corruption and spills blood? While we glorify, praise and sanctify You?' He said, 'I know what you do not know.*'"[26]

Know the attribute of humanity and the attribute of the angels. The angels looked upon the nature of Adam and found in it anger and lust, as well as intellect ('*aql*); but they knew that Allāh had not ordained anything of good except in his intellect and perceived that the two negative forces would dominate the intellect of Adam. Anger carries him to the shedding of blood while lust carries him to corruption.

But the intellect is stronger than the two passions. Allāh has indeed placed in mankind lust, the force of anger, connivance, and deception – the same as the devils. But He also placed in him the propensity for clarity through using his intellect, similar to the angels. He who becomes mired in lusts until he becomes interested in nothing but food, clothes, and satisfying his passions; the destruction becomes realized on him. "*Indeed, they are like cattle, nay, but they are even further astray.*"[27] And he who obeys the force of anger until he comes to give himself free reign and thereby does harm; as with one who has followed his lusts, he has left the very limit of humanity. Such

24 Qur'ān, 12:21.

25 This is a variation of the Qur'ān: "And Allāh is not incapacitated by anything in the heavens or in the earth" (35:44).

26 Qur'ān, 2:30.

27 Qur'ān, 25:44.

men have surely lost their humanity, whatever that was, until they have become a type of beast or devil.

The trait of intellect has remained in the son of Adam if he makes use of the worship of Allāh, and the (intellect's) clarity for drawing near to Allāh. He then arrives at the knowledge (*ma'rifa*) of Allāh and becomes of the species of the angels or better than some of the angels. And with this Allāh has described (the two types of) man with His words, "*They are the worst of creation*" and "*They are the best of creation*."[28] The man of His first description is certainly the worst of creation, and the man of His second description is certainly the best of creation. If the servant has inclined to good, and does nothing but good, Allāh turns him toward (his further) advantage, and adds from Himself until he becomes from among the best of creation. And if he is from the other side, Allāh capitalizes on his depravity and adds misguidance to him until he becomes from among the worst of creation.

Our religion calls for the revival of the interminable, eternal spiritual existence, achieved through the proper use of the human form internally and externally in following the command and avoiding the abominations, and drowning the heart in the remembrance (*dhikr*) of Allāh.

The creation is of three categories: a complete, unlimited category that will never be lacking; a category that will never attain completion; and a category sometimes complete and sometimes lacking. As for the first category, these are the angels. They lack nothing in any state among the states of being. The category that will never touch perfection is the animals and plants. It is mankind who is sometimes complete and sometimes lacking. Completion or perfection is not in his essence, because if it were in his essence, he would continue to retain perfection. But it is only so long as he remembers

---

28 Qur'ān, 98:6-7.

Allāh in his heart and with his tongue that he is complete. And whenever he becomes heedless of the remembrance of Allāh, he is lacking.

So it is always incumbent on the servant to remember Allāh. We have been commanded to pray because it constitutes the remembrance of Allāh. "*Establish the prayer for (the sake of) My remembrance.*"[29] Fasting, alms giving, and pilgrimage – all of these acts of worship call the servant (back) to the remembrance of Allāh. The remembrance of Allāh is the highest degree in the religion. (And in the verse of the Qur᾽ān beginning with) "*Indeed the men and women who submit*" to "*the men and women who remember Allāh much*,"[30] Allāh has mentioned those who remember in the last or highest of the degrees because the remembrance of Allāh is the opening up of sainthood. So whoever remembers Allāh, he is among the saints of Allāh, and who is heedless of the Truth is with the devils.

And for this, we praise Allāh for what is from and with Him: the blessing of faith; and a sufficient blessing it is. Praise be to Allāh for the blessing of the Qur᾽ān, and praise be to Allāh on account of our master Muḥammad, and praise be to Allāh who gave us in this end of time the path of those who remember, the path of Shaykh Aḥmad Tijānī. Surely we see all those who hold to it guarding the rules of Islam and the Sunnah of the Messenger, and asking for knowledge and goodness, and guarding the remembrance of Allāh.

The awe or fear of Allāh (*taqwā*) is the servant's guarantee for the entirety of his needs in this world and the next. If the servant wants knowledge, let him fear Allāh. The Most High has said, "*Fear Allāh and Allāh will teach you.*"[31] If he desires sainthood, Allāh has said, "*Indeed, His saints are none but those who are in awe (of Him).*"[32] If he wants Paradise, Allāh, may he

29 Qur᾽ān, 20:14.
30 Qur᾽ān, 33:35.
31 Qur᾽ān, 2:282.
32 Qur᾽ān, 8:34.

be praised and exalted, says, "*A Paradise as vast as the heavens and the earth, (prepared) for those who are in awe (of Him).*"[33] To those who desire the love of Allāh, Allāh says, "*Allāh surely loves those who are in awe (of Him).*"[34] To those who desire the (good) end, Allāh says, "*The (good) end is for the those who are in awe (of Him).*"[35] To those who want safety from the plotting of connivers, Allāh says, "*If you are patient and in awe (of Me), their plotting will in no way harm you.*"[36] If he desires safety from hardships or wants provision, Allāh says, "*Whoever is in awe of Allāh, He will provide a way out and provide for him from where he never imagined.*"[37] If he wants ease in his affairs, Allāh says, "*Whoever is in awe of Allāh, He makes ease in his affairs.*"[38] If he wants safety from the Fire, Allāh says, "*Then we save those who are in awe (of Allāh).*"[39] If he wants honor before Allāh, Allāh says, "*Surely the most honorable before Allāh are those among you who are in awe (of Him).*"[40] All the needs of the servant are subsumed in *taqwā*. So I advise you with *taqwā*, and it is obedience to the commands and avoidance of the abominations.

I praise Allāh for permitting me the opportunity to visit a man (Muḥammad al-Hāfiz[41]) who is without doubt an inheritor (*khalīfa*) of the Shaykh, my master Aḥmad Tijānī, and whose description matches the Shaykh's, as I myself know him

33 Qur'ān, 3:133.
34 Qur'ān, 9:4.
35 Qur'ān, 28:83.
36 Qur'ān, 3:120.
37 Qur'ān, 65:2-3.
38 Qur'ān, 65:4.
39 Qur'ān, 19:72.
40 Qur'ān, 49:13.
41 Shaykh Muḥammad al-Ḥāfiẓ al-Miṣrī (d. 1979) was a renowned Ḥadīth scholar in Egypt and the head Tijānī shaykh in the country. Shaykh Ibrāhīm and Shaykh al-Ḥāfiẓ were close friends and remained in correspondence, as evidenced by Shaykh Ḥasan Cissé's quotation from a letter from Shaykh al-Ḥāfiẓ in his "Revivalist of the Sunnah" in the beginning of the present book.

to be. Indeed, when I look at him, it is as if I am looking at my master Aḥmad Tijānī. By his presence, I found the opportunity of meeting with these brothers, the companions of the Shaykh, and all of the companions of the Shaykh are saints. Indeed the saints of Allāh are the ones working with Allāh, and their love is a guarantee of happiness in this world and the next. The Messenger of Allāh has guaranteed for Shaykh Aḥmad Tijānī that all of his companions will be saints,[42] so it is incumbent, if Allāh wills, that you realize this guarantee.

We look to those who remember Allāh, those who guard the Law, for they are the community of saints. They are people whose companionship will never bring unhappiness. And I thank you all for this reception and for the love for the sake of Allāh. My hope is for this love for myself and for you, that we may be among those about whom the Ḥadīth narrates: "Allāh has servants who are not prophets or martyrs, but whom the prophets and martyrs envy for their proximity to the Real on the Day of Judgment, and they are those who gather for the sake of Allāh."[43] I ask Allāh to make us among the elite companions of the Shaykh, and that He inspire in us the pure desire for His grace and pleasure.

Peace upon you all and the mercy of Allāh.

---

42 As recorded by ʿAlī Ḥarāzim in the *Jawāhir al-maʿānī*, Shaykh Aḥmad Tijānī reported that the Prophet Muḥammad informed in a waking vision that anybody who loves him is a beloved of the Prophet himself, and will not die until he has become a saint. See Ḥarāzim, *Jawāhir al-maʿānī* (Beruit: Dār al-Fikr, 2001), 54. As Shaykh Ibrāhīm here indicates, it is up to the aspirant to realize the guarantee, for Shaykh Aḥmad Tijānī himself warned that the disciple should not "take the promise of salvation as a trick to stave off the punishment of Allāh for his sins ... his heart must be ever fearful of the punishment of Allāh" (*Jawāhir al-maʿānī*, 56).

43 Ḥadīth on the authority of Amr ibn Abasa and related by al-Ṭabarānī. A slightly different version is that on the authority of Muʿadh ibn Jabal and related by al-Tirmidhī, where the envied ones are those who love each other for Allāh's sake.

The Stations of the Religion

Shaykh Ibrāhīm drafted the following letter concerning the "three stations of the religion" (maqāmāt al-dīn al-thalāth) on his farm outside of Kaolack in 1931.[44] It has since served as a significant public description of the steps of spiritual wayfaring (sulūk).

* * *

In the Name of Allāh, the Compassionate, the Merciful, and may Allāh's blessing be upon His noble Prophet Muḥammad, the best of humanity, and upon his companions, the stars (of guidance).

All praise is due to Allāh, the Peace, the Security, the Beneficent, glory be to Him. He is the King, the Forgiving, the Merciful, the Watchful, the Protector.

Peace be upon (Muḥammad) the straight path, the God-conscious one, the pure, the truthful, the sincere, the one molded with tremendous character, the observant, the witness,

44 Niasse, *Jawāhir al-rasā'il*, III: 50-55.

the source of most perfect gnosis, the servant (ʿabd) and the master (*sayyid*), the one described with the attributes of the Greatest Master. May Allāh's complete satisfaction be upon the helper of the Truth by the Truth, the guide to the straight path, and on his people, (may this prayer be) worthy of his merit, and surely his worth is exceedingly great.

I have received your noble letter and greetings of peace, most agreeable beloved and exemplary seeker of (Divine) satisfaction, ʿUmar b. Mālik, may the Sovereign treat both you and your father with kindness. I received your question concerning the three stations of the Religion (*maqāmāt al-dīn*), the abodes that pertain to them, and the reality of these properties. This matter has been discussed with extensive research by the master, the knower of Allāh, ʿUbayda b. Anjūba, in his book *Mīzāb* (*al-raḥma*).[45] But since you did not find what suffices you therein, here is what has been possible for me to write down of my thoughts:

There is nothing worthy of worship but Allāh (*lā ilāha ill-Allāh*). The stations of the Religion are three: submission (*islām*), faith (īmān), and excellence (*iḥsān*). *Islām* is the pronouncement of "There is nothing worthy of worship but Allāh." Īmān is to have knowledge of "There is nothing worthy of worship but Allāh." *Iḥsān* is the course in accordance with "There is nothing worthy of worship but Allāh." This means that you pronounce the words of a spiritual state, the speech of Allāh, the noble word; which is the word of repentance, the word of God-consciousness, the word of sincerity, the word of Divine Unity, the good word. This (statement) has three degrees. The first degree is the station of *Islām*, which is undertaking the emulation of the wise statement on this lowest plane of material existence (*ḥaḍra al-nāsūt*). The second degree, Īmān, is

---

45 Further discussion of Ibn Anjūba's discussion of the *Maqāmāt al-dīn* can be found in Rüdiger Seesemann, *The Divine Flood: Ibrāhīm Niasse and the Roots of a Twentieth-Century Sufi Revival* (Oxford UP, 2010), 87-91.

the knowledge of this statement, and the third degree, *Iḥsān*, is (being) the speech of Allāh. Thus the three stations can be explained as all revolving around the statement, "There is nothing worthy of worship but Allāh."

Repentance

As for the "abodes" (*manāzil*), the first abode of Islām is repentance (*tawba*). This means removing oneself from denying blessing. Having gratitude and consideration for every blessing is a means of attaining the satisfaction of the Benefactor, and the opposite of gratitude is disbelief (*kufr*). The Sufi scholars have added that repentance is leaving aside base character traits for sublime character traits. I would add that base character traits for the common people include leaving aside the obligations of the Religion (*farāʾiḍ*) and pursuing forbidden things. The baseness of the elite is to leave aside the supererogatory exemplary acts (*faḍāʾil*) while pursuing reprehensible things (*makrūhāt*). The baseness of the elite of the elite is the turning away from the Divine Presence (*ḥaḍra*), which constitutes heedlessness.

This form of repentance is the reality of repentance, because real repentance means to kill the lower self (*nafs*), as the Most High said, *"So repent to your Creator, and kill your (lower) selves."*[46] (True repentance is when) one does not perceive the repentance, nor perceive anything belonging to it; neither action, nor spiritual station, nor station. This is repentance from repentance: "*Surely Allāh loves the repentant.*"[47] In other words, (those who repent) from repentance.

---

46 Qurʾān, 2:54.
47 Qurʾān, 2:222.

Steadfastness

The second (abode of Islām) is steadfastness (*istiqāma*), which means traveling (*sulūk*) the straight path without deviation from the structure of the path. Allāh, Blessed and Exalted is He, enumerated ten qualities of the straight path in the "Chapter of the Cattle (Sūra*t al-An*ʿā*m*) by His statement:

> *Say, "Come, I will recite that which your Lord has made a sacred duty on you: that you do not associate anything as a partner with Him, that you be good to your parents; that you do not kill your children because of poverty – it is We who provide for you and them; that you do not approach shameful deeds, whether openly or secretly; and that you do not take human life which Allāh has made sacred, except in the course of legal justice. This He has commanded you, so that you may discern.*
>
> *Do not come near to the orphan's property, except to improve it, until he reaches maturity. Give full measure and weight, in justice. We do not burden any soul beyond its capacity. And if you give your word, do justice to it, even though it be (against) a kinsman; and fulfill the covenant of Allāh. This He has commanded you, so that you may remember.*
>
> *Verily this is My straight path, so follow it. Do not follow other ways, they will sever you from His way.*[48]

So the goal of the straight path as designated is action, putting in practice these properties. The first is not associating partners with Allāh; then not taking the life Allāh has made sacred, not killing one's children fearing poverty, abandoning shameful deeds whether openly or secretly, and so forth. The

48 Qurʾān, 6:151-153.

steadfastness of the common folk is thus fulfilling the rights of the straight path.

For the elite, steadfastness is traveling the straight path, while the Messenger of Allāh, peace and blessings upon him, is with them. So this means annihilation in the Prophet, along with (annihilation in) loving him and his character, thus molding oneself with his character, both openly and secretly. This entails busying oneself with his remembrance, invoking blessings on him, and praying for him in every breath. This is the steadfastness mentioned in the statement of the Most High, "*Those who say our Lord is Allāh, and are steadfast, the Angels descend on them, saying, 'Do not fear nor grieve, but listen to the good tidings of the Paradise promised you.*"[49]

The steadfastness of the elite of the elite is that nothing of the creation persists in you, even if concealed; and what is repulsive (*khabīth*) is completely unknown. This steadfastness is more comprehensive than the general steadfastness, since normally affairs fall into various categories: obligatory, preferred, neutral, disliked, and forbidden.

God-consciousness

The third (abode of Islām) is the fear of Allāh (*taqwā*), which means carrying out the commandments and avoiding the prohibitions, openly and secretly, publicly and privately. So complete implementation of the commandments and complete avoidance of the prohibitions is the fear of the common folk. Among the elite, fear of Allāh is to remember Him and not to forget Him, to obey Him and not to disobey Him. The Most High said, "*O you who believe, fear Allāh as He should be feared.*"[50] This refers to the degree of the elite (in God-con-

49 Qur'ān, 41:30.
50 Qur'ān, 3:102.

sciousness), just as the Most High's statement, "*Fear Allāh as much as you can*,"[51] refers to the degree of the common folk.

The fear of the elite of the elite is when nothing occurs to the mind except by Allāh even for a single moment. The gnostic says, "If other than You should occur to my mind, it is a selfish desire afflicting my thought, heedlessly, for which I would be guilty of apostasy (*ridda*)." But this is the spiritual state (*ḥāl*) of the gnostic and the spiritual station (*maqām*) of the unique and comprehensive saintly pole (*al-quṭb al-fard al-jāmiʿ*). The poet is here speaking of his spiritual state, but this (permanent) state of mind is not incumbent on the (ordinary) gnostic. This type of fear is alluded to in Allāh's saying, "*Surely Allāh loves the God-fearing*."[52]

Truthfulness

The second station of the Religion is the station of Īmān (faith). Its first abode is truthfulness (*ṣidq*), which is working righteousness seeking the Countenance of Allāh the Most High. He said:

> *Righteousness is having faith in Allāh, the Last Day, the Angels, the Scripture, and the Prophets; and to give of your wealth, for love of Him, to your kin, to the needy, to the traveler, to those who ask, and for freeing slaves; and to establish the prayer and to pay the poor-due; and to fulfill the contracts you have made; and to be patient in tribulation, adversity, and time of stress. Such are the truthful ones.*[53]

Such is the truthfulness of the common folk.

---

51 Qurʾān, 64:16.

52 Qurʾān, 3:76.

53 Qurʾān, 2:177.

The truthfulness of the elite is the truthfulness in the love of Allāh's Exalted Essential Being (*al-dhāt al-ʿaliyya*). Arrival to the Exalted Essential Being becomes more beloved to him than everything in existence, and Allāh's Name is more beloved to him than any name, and Allāh's Speech is more beloved than any other words, and Allāh's satisfaction is more beloved to him than any other satisfaction, and Allāh's beloveds (*aḥbāb*) are more beloved to him than his own beloveds. So this is the truthfulness of the elite, and the Most High said, "*Be among the truthful ones.*"[54] The person who has attained this station does not attach his mind to the love of anything unless Allāh desires that he find it. The mind of the truthful person does not become attached to anything that Allāh does not want to exist for him. "*And that is the bounty of Allāh, which He gives to whom He wills, and Allāh is the possessor of great bounty.*"[55]

The truthfulness of the elite of the elite is to attest (*taṣdīq*) to everything conveyed to the Prophetic Presence from the Divine Presence; whether knowledge, spiritual state, secrets, conduct, rights, or duties. Whoever attains truthfulness to this degree possesses the best form of truthfulness.

Sincerity

The second (abode of faith) is sincerity (*ikhlāṣ*). Sincerity is to act upon the commandments and to forsake the prohibitions for the sake of Allāh's Noble Countenance, for if you find in yourself any ostentation, concern for reputation, or vanity, you have not attained sincerity. This is the sincerity of the common folk.

54 Qurʾān, 9:119.
55 Qurʾān, 57:21.

The sincerity of the elite is to put the Religion into practice, not for the sake of reward, nor for fear of punishment, nor for attaining to a spiritual station (*maqām*). Rather, you worship Allāh out of yearning (for Him). Worship (*ʿubūdiyya*) means that you put the Religion into practice for no other reason than the fact Allāh deserves to be worshipped, and you are a servant for whom nothing else is fitting besides service. So you act for His sake, and you do not perceive yourself deserving anything from Him. You give witness to the blessing, and He gives witness to your good deeds. Indeed, such deeds are from Him to you. He created them, and attributed them to you from His grace and blessing.

The sincerity of the elite of the elite is to banish all otherness in your dealing with the Real (*al-Ḥaqq*), and surely your own self (*nafs*) is among the otherness so banished. Like this you will perceive that all works (ʿamal) are from Allāh, to Allāh, and by Allāh. You have no entry in them and no exit from them. Know that Allāh loves (such) sincere ones.

Tranquility

The third (abode of faith) is tranquility (*ṭumaʾnīna*). Tranquility is the stillness of the heart with Allāh, its sufficiency in Allāh from everything else, and its dwelling (*baqā*ʾ) with Allāh. Youthful speculations as to what will benefit or harm the self no longer exist in the heart. Rather the soul (*nafs*) has become calm in Allāh's Hands. The tongue of this spiritual state says, "O Allāh, on You is my reliance..."[56] This is the meaning of tranquility, but it is not possible except for the

56 This is a reference to an important supplication of the Tijāniyya order (see Muḥammad al-Ḥāfiẓ al-Tijānī, *Aḥzāb wa awrād* (Dakar: al-Maktaba al-Islāmiyya, unknown date), 139-140) used by Shaykh Ibrāhīm Niasse for the spiritual training (*tarbiya*) of disciples. See the section on supplications later in this book.

elite. The tranquility of the elite of the elite consists in their certain knowledge that there is nothing other than Allāh in existence. The soul of such a person does not rest except in Him, and does not return except to Him, and its address from Allāh is "*O soul in tranquility, return to Your Lord.*"[57]

Awareness

The third station of the Religion is spiritual excellence (*iḥsān*). Its first abode is awareness (*murāqaba*), which is continuous presence with Allāh. The knowledge gained by His acquaintance permeates the entirety of the servant, so that this notion (of Divine proximity) never leaves him. The reality is disclosed to him from behind a subtle veil, so he gains experiential understanding. The one who arrives to this station may speak words that do not reflect the perfect specification of the spiritually arrived, for he has not fully arrived since the reality is disclosed to him from behind a subtle veil. He takes knowledge by means of understanding and experience, not direct witnessing. So this is the awareness of the elite before witnessing. The awareness after witnessing is the awareness of the elite of the elite. This awareness is most precious, and is a station among the stations of the spiritually distinguished (*al-rijāl*), the result of gnosis.

Witnessing

The second (abode of *iḥsān*) is witnessing (*mushāhada*), which is the ocular vision of the Real by the Real, without misgiving, doubt, or delusion. This is because nothing remains except the Real, by the Real, in the Real. So long as a single hair of the servant should remain in existence, he will not arrive

57 Qur'ān, 89:27-28.

to this station. Nay, he must pass away from himself, from all otherness and concern for what is other. The tongue of this spiritual state says, "Nothing remains except Allāh, nothing other than Him; so there is no object of arrival, and nothing to be made clear." Here there is no name and no description, no designation and no delimitation. This vision is without explanation, and it has no differentiation and no union, no direction and no reception, no beginning, no connection, and no separation. There is no remembrance, no one performing the remembrance, and no object of remembrance. "*Truth has come and falsehood has perished. Surely falsehood is ever bound to perish.*"[58]

This degree is the closest of degrees to the spiritual opening (*fatḥ*), and what came before this was not by such opening. Witnessing is the door of gnosis (*maʿrifa*), but it is not gnosis. Every gnostic has been opened, but not every opened one is a gnostic.

Gnosis

The third (abode of *iḥsān*) is gnosis (*maʿrifa*), which is when the spirit becomes thoroughly familiar with and fixed in the presence of (Divine) witnessing, with complete annihilation (*fanāʾ*) and subsequent remaining (*baqāʾ*) by Allāh. The gnostic according to the Sufis is the one who either sees otherness as the Essence (*ʿayn*), or who witnesses the Real in otherness. But the gnostic with me is the one who finds annihilation once in the Divine Essence (*dhāt*), and in the Attribute two or three times. So he finds annihilation in the Name once, and bears witness to the existence through the three (Attributed) Realities, bearing witness to the Names by the Name. This is a station that would require stripping the thorn-bush of its leaves and the shredding of internal organs, but it is not

58 Qurʾān, 17:81.

obtained by sacrifice of wealth and children.[59] The resident of this station is completely awake to Allāh, His wisdom and His rulings. He is content with the manifestation of the decrees of Divine ordainment. He has obtained a perfect contentment with Allāh, so Allāh is contented with him. His soul (*nafs*) is thus worthy of being addressed by the words of the Most High: "*So enter the company of My (honored) servants, and enter My Paradise.*"[60]

Gnosis is the last station of the Religion while repentance (*tawba*) is the first. Even still, repentance is better than gnosis since (true) repentance is the result of gnosis. This is because the reality of repentance is to be absent from repentance. For this reason Shaykh Tijānī, the Seal of Saints, may Allāh be pleased with him, used to say, "I swear by Allāh – other than whom there is no god – I did not reach the station of repentance (*maqām al-tawba*)." He meant, may Allāh be pleased with him, that he had repented from seeing his own repentance, for so long as the servant sees the repentance belonging to himself, he has not reached the station of repentance…

The reality of repentance is the repentance from repentance, for "surely Allāh is He who accepts repentance, the Merciful."[61]

The reality of steadfastness (*istiqāma*) is the remaining (*baqā'*) after annihilation (*fanā'*): "*Verily, Allāh ordains what He wills.*"[62]

59 In other words, it is a station only obtained through Allāh's favor. I thank Moctar Ba for relating to me the interpretation of this sentence from Shaykh Baye Ould al-Haiba, interview, Medina-Baye Senegal, 3 January, 2015.

60 Qur'ān, 89:30.

61 Qur'ān, 9:104.

62 Qur'ān, 5:1.

The reality of fear (*taqwā*) is the absence of thought unless it comes from the Divine Mind (*al-khāṭir*), even for a single moment: "*That is because Allāh is the Real.*"[63]

The reality of truthfulness (*ṣidq*) is the singular devotion to Allāh: "*Everything will perish except His Countenance.*"[64]

The reality of sincerity (*ikhlāṣ*) is that you do not see good deeds proceeding from you, returning to you, or being owned by you. Whatever is in the heavens and earth is from Him. "*To Him return all affairs.*"[65] "His is the sovereignty, to Him belongs all praise."[66]

The reality of tranquility (*ṭumaʾnīna*) is that you do not wish for the end of what is, nor the existence of what is not. "*Surely Allāh knows and you do not know.*"[67] "*He is not asked about what He does.*"[68]

The reality of awareness (*murāqaba*) is the ceaseless attachment of the heart to Allāh. "*Verily, your Lord is ever watchful.*"[69] "*And there is no affair in which you are engaged, no portion of the Qurʾān which you recite, and no deed that you are doing, except that We are witness over you while you are engaged in it.*"[70] "*And We know what his soul whispers to him, for We are closer to him than his jugular vein.*"[71] "*There is no secret council of three except that He is the fourth of them.*"[72] "*Surely Allāh is the one knowledgeable of what is in the hearts.*"[73]

---

63 Qurʾān, 31:30.
64 Qurʾān, 28:88.
65 Qurʾān, 42:53.
66 Qurʾān, 64:1.
67 Qurʾān, 16:74.
68 Qurʾān, 21:23.
69 Qurʾān, 89:14.
70 Qurʾān, 10:61.
71 Qurʾān, 50:16.
72 Qurʾān, 58:7.
73 Qurʾān, 3:154.

The reality of witnessing (*mushāhada*) is the vision of the Real with the eyes: "*Everywhere you turn, there is the Countenance of Allāh.*"[74]

The reality of gnosis (*maʿrifa*) is the direct witnessing of the perfection of the Divine Being (*al-kamāl al-dhātī*). "*There is nothing like to Him.*"[75]

74 Qurʾān, 2:115.
75 Qurʾān, 42:11.

The Knowledge of Allāh

The following was a lengthy public speech delivered in the Islamic Republic of Mauritania in 1968.[76] *I have omitted the introductory formalities normally included in such a public address.*

* * *

Every community (*jamāʿa*) has a reason that brings them together. As for us, our companionship is for the sake of Allāh, blessed and exalted is He, and for the sake of His Religion. As you know, if the companionship (*ṣuḥba*) is leading to a goal of which the members of the community have not yet come to know, whoever leads them must know the path, and he must also walk on this path. If they desire companionship, they will walk behind him so that they do not go astray from the path. This being the case, companionship is a tangible reality. If one of us moves, and others sit down, or if some of us set out on the path and some go off the path: this is not companionship. So we hope that our companionship is a reality, and that you strive not to become divided. Be brothers in this world, and brothers in the afterlife.

76 Niasse, *Jawāhir al-rasāʾil*, II: 54-70.

I advise you and myself with the fear of Allāh (*taqwā*) in secret and in public. This advice will guarantee all your needs in the world, in the religion, and in the afterlife. The fear of Allāh is the key to all the servant's needs in this world and the next, those apparent and those hidden. The first thing the believing servant requires is knowledge. The fear of Allāh is the key to knowledge. The Most High said, "And fear Allāh and Allāh will teach you, and Allāh has knowledge of all things."[77] So whoever wants knowledge, let him fear Allāh the Most High. In this vein, (Imam Muḥammad) al-Shāfiʿī said, "I complained to (my teacher) Wakīʿ (b. Jarrah) about my poor memory, so he guided me to abandon disobedience. He told me that knowledge was light, and the light of Allāh is not given to the sinful person." Whoever wants knowledge, let him fear Allāh, blessed and exalted is He.

The fear of Allāh means to carry out the commandments and avoid the prohibitions, both openly and secretly. In other words, the fear of Allāh means being afraid to leave aside what Allāh has obligated on you, and to be afraid of doing something that He has prohibited you. Indeed, avoid the opposite: carrying out what Allāh has prohibited and refraining from what He has commanded. The fear of Allāh is the guarantee for all the servant's hopes, even if he is seeking sainthood (*wilāya*), to be among the friends (*awliyāʾ*) of Allāh the Blessed and Exalted. He said, "For surely the friends of Allāh have no anxiety (*khawf*) or sadness, those who believe and fear Allāh."[78] On this subject, Abū Ḥanīfa[79] said, "If the scholars (ʿulamāʾ) who act on their knowledge are not the friends of Allāh the Most High, then Allāh does not have any friend." Whoever believes in Allāh, carries out the commandments and avoids the prohibitions, he is among the friends of Allāh the Most High, those

77 Qurʾān, 2:282.

78 Qurʾān, 10:62-63.

79 Nuʿmān b. Thābit, known as Abū Ḥanīfa (d. 767, Baghdad), was the founder of the Ḥanafī school of Sunni jurisprudence.

who have no anxiety or sadness: no anxiety in this world and no sadness in the afterlife. Perhaps the servant wants to have the glad tidings in the life of this world and in the next that they are indeed the friends of Allāh.

The Messenger of Allāh, may Allāh's peace and blessing be upon him, was once asked, "Who are they who have no anxiety or sadness?" The Noble Messenger said, "They are people among people who gather together for the sake of Allāh, they sit together for the sake of Allāh, and they visit each other for the sake of Allāh. They are those who have no anxiety or sadness. These are servants who are not Prophets nor martyrs, but the Prophets and martyrs envy them for their closeness to the Real on the Day of Resurrection."

Love for the sake of Allāh is a tremendous affair. I bear witness to you that I love you all for the sake of Allāh, and that you love me for the sake of Allāh. Surely Allāh the Blessed and Exalted has servants that He will shade on the Day when there will be no shade except His shade. He will shade them beneath the shade of His throne. There are seven types of such servants: the just imam; a youth who develops in obedience to Allāh the Blessed and Exalted; a person whose heart remains attached to the mosque from when he leaves it until he returns to it; a man who refuses the invitation of a beautiful woman, saying, "I fear Allāh"; a man who remembers Allāh freely until his eyes overflow with tears; a man who gives in charity secretly with his right hand so that his left is not aware; and two persons who love each other for the sake of Allāh the Blessed and Exalted.[80] Love is the easiest of these characteristics to have, and it is the best. A man is with whom he loves, and who loves a people gathers with them. As the Messenger said, "Surely a man is with whom he loves." Anas said, "We were never so happy in

80 The Shaykh is here paraphrasing the well-known ḥadīth related by Abū Hurayra, found in the collections Bukhārī and Muslim, "There are seven whom Allāh will shade on a Day when there is no shade but His ..."

Islam as the day the Messenger said, 'A man is with whom he loves.' And I bear witness that I love the Messenger of Allāh, and I love Abū Bakr and ʿUmar." Praise be to Allāh, we also love them. We love a man when we come to realize he is not of the people of the Fire. The statement, "a man is with whom he loves," is the highest hope we have for ourselves and for our loved ones.

The fear of Allāh is the key to Paradise. "*And the Paradise ... is promised to the God-fearing.*"[81] The fear of Allāh is the safety from Hellfire. "*Then we save the God-fearing.*"[82] The fear of Allāh is the cause of a praiseworthy ending. "*And the good ending is for the God-fearing.*"[83] The fear of Allāh is an escape from constraints and the key to provision. "*Whoever fears Allāh, He makes for them a way out and provides from them from where he does not expect.*"[84] The fear of Allāh is the key to ease. "*Whoever fears Allāh, He makes his affair easy for him.*"[85] The fear of Allāh is the cause for assistance. "*And if you are patient and fear Allāh, their plots will not harm you in the least.*"[86] All that we are seeking in this world or the next, as well as in the religion, is found in the fear of Allāh. So I advise you and myself with the fear of Allāh privately and publicly, which entails carrying out the commandments and avoiding the prohibitions externally and internally.

The Most High said, "*Fear Allāh and seek the means of approach to Him.*"[87] If you want to be God-fearing, you must have a means by which you are brought to the purity of this state. There are three such means mentioned in the Qurʾān. The first is the emulation of Allāh's Messenger, may the peace and bless-

---

81 Qurʾān, 3:133.
82 Qurʾān, 19:72.
83 Qurʾān, 28:73.
84 Qurʾān, 65:3.
85 Qurʾān, 65:4.
86 Qurʾān, 3:120.
87 Qurʾān, 5:35.

ing of Allāh be upon him, in the entirety of words and deeds. This is a means by which the servant arrives to Allāh the Blessed and Exalted. "*Say, 'If you love Allāh, follow me and Allāh will love you.'*"[88] And the Noble Messenger used to say, "If you love Allāh, follow me." So who follows the Messenger in entirety of his deeds and statements will achieve this love of Allāh for His servant. Allāh said in another narration, "When I love him, I become him." If Allāh loves a servant, He becomes his hearing, his sight, his tongue, his hand, and his foot. This is the beginning of sainthood, and thus the best of means.

The second means of approach to Allāh is the Qur᾿ān. Those who perform this remembrance of Allāh the Blessed and Exalted have no ambition except His Countenance. The Most High said, "*Restrain yourself with those who call to their Lord by day and night, desiring His Countenance.*"[89] Confine yourself with the people who remember Allāh morning and evening, not desiring anything except the Countenance of Allāh the Blessed and Exalted. This, then, is a means of connecting the servant to Allāh the Blessed and Exalted.

The third means of approaching the Divine is the companionship with the gnostic of Allāh the Blessed and Exalted. The Most High said, "*And follow the way of him who turns to Me.*"[90] The one who turns to Allāh in all of his states is the gnostic of Allāh: there is nothing with him except Allāh. This is also true for the one who accompanies him, finding the gnostic the means to connect himself to Allāh the Blessed and Exalted. The universe in reality has nothing in it except Allāh the Blessed and Exalted. This is the same for the human being as it is for the universe.

A person desires arrival to Allāh, but finds a veil between himself and Allāh. This veil is only the creation. If he should

88 Qur᾿ān, 3:31.
89 Qur᾿ān, 18:28.
90 Qur᾿ān, 31:15.

persist in the remembrance of Allāh the Blessed and Exalted, making his heart present to Allāh, the creation will vanish from him, and he will arrive to Allāh the Blessed and Exalted. The creation becomes "*like the mirage in a desert, which the thirsty man mistakes for water until he comes upon it and finds nothing, and instead he finds Allāh with him.*"[91] The Greatest Shaykh, Ibn al-ʿArabī al-Ḥātimī said, "Whoever sees the creation as a mirage, he has lifted the veil."

If the aspirant should come to the perfected shaykh desiring arrival to Allāh the Blessed and Exalted, the shaykh will first occupy him with the remembrance of Allāh the Blessed and Exalted until he becomes connected with the presence of Allāh the Blessed and Exalted by way of annihilation (*fanā*ʾ). Should the servant not annihilate himself in the Essence of Allāh, he has not completed his faith. If the veil should remain with him here, (he should beware) of a type of punishment (inevitably) overtaking the servant. As the Most High has said "Nay, on that Day they will be veiled from their Lord, then they will indeed enter the Hellfire."[92] So whenever the veil arrives, there arrives the punishment. But if the servant continues with the remembrance (*dhikr*) of Allāh, he attains extinction (*fanā*ʾ). And extinction is of three types: extinction in the Works (of Allāh), extinction in the Attributes, and extinction in the Essence.

Many of the believers reach the stage of extinction in the Works. Whoever knows that there is no actor in the existence except Allāh; that is the completion of (the servant's) extinction in the works, for he knows that there is no actor except Allāh. Many believers are able to arrive to this station. I say to the students in my grammar lesson[93]: "The grammarians say,

---

91 Qurʾān, 24:39.

92 Qurʾān, 83:15-16.

93 Shaykh Ibrāhīm Niasse was of course a renowned Arabic linguist, and gave grammar (*nahw*) lessons himself. He also authored a book on grammar, *Tuhfat al-Atfal fi haqa'iq al-af'al fi al-sarf* ("The treasure of the

'The verbal subject (*fā'il*) in reality is Allāh, even if He engenders the action metaphorically by means of an agent, for one who engenders the action is inseparable from the action performed. And all of this (subject, agent, and action) is Allāh, because the doer (*fā'il*) is in reality Allāh, and the metaphorical agent, who they say engenders the action, is also Allāh.'" Who knows that there is no actor except Allāh, attains extinction (*fanā*') in the presence (*ḥaḍra*) of Allāh's Works, and has here found some of the (true) faith (required).

But if he extinguishes himself in the Attributes (of Allāh), he ascends from this station. The Attributes of Allāh are well known among all of us, they can be read in the beginning of any book on the Oneness (of Allāh)[94]: power, will, knowledge, life, hearing, sight, speech. These are the attributes of Allāh, and when we leave them for Allāh alone, we arrive to the extinction in the Attributes, knowing there is no power except that it belongs to Allāh. Indeed, the scholars have settled for us in their elementary teaching on the subject that power, for example, is of the attributes of Allāh the Most High. Likewise, there is no will except that is it belongs to Allāh, and there is no life except that it belongs to Allāh, and no knowledge except that belonging to Allāh, and no hearing except that belonging to Allāh, and no sight except that belonging to Allāh, and no speech except that belonging to Allāh. Who has knowledge of this finds extinction in the Attributes.

---

children concerning the real meanings of verbs in conjugation"). Published in Nouakchott, Mauritania, by Muahmmad Salim Mawlud; and in Beirut (Dar al-Fikr) as part of ʿAbd-Allāh ibn Muḥammad Fodio's *al-Hisn al-rasin fi 'ilm al-sarf*. See Seesemann, *Nach der Flut*, 909.

94 Shaykh Ibrāhīm is here referring to the subject of *'aqīda*, or the doctrine of Allāh's Oneness. The primary work studied in West Africa (as elsewhere in the Islamic world) concerning this branch of the Islamic sciences, to which the Shaykh is likely here referring, is the ʿ*Aqīda al-sughrā* of Muḥammad b. Yusuf al-Sanusi (d. 1490, Algeria).

If the servant ascends (from this station), he finds extinction (*fanā'*) in the Essence (of Allāh). All things go from him until nothing remains except Allāh. The tongue of his state then says: "Nothing remains except Allāh, nothing besides Him. So there is not in this place any attachment or intelligibility."

In this state is found the statement, "There is no god but Allāh." But for this statement there is a shell, and an essence (*lubb*), and an essence of the essence. The shell is the doctrine of Unity known by the common folk, "There is no god but Allāh", found in the Qur'ān: "*Allāh, there is no god but Him.*"[95] But this, in truth, is for him who has been absent from Allāh. Allāh the Most High is never absent; you are the only absent one.

If a person persists in the journey and directs himself to Allāh, he arrives to the station of attendance with Allāh, and addresses Him as He is addressed in the ritual prayer: "*You we worship and You we ask for help, lead us to the straight path.*"[96] Here he has arrived to the station of "There is no god but You," and that as well is a remembrance found in the Qur'ān: "*There is no god but You.*"[97]

If the aspirant completes his journey, he becomes extinguished in the Essence (*dhāt*) of Allāh, where he does not find any remembrance except, "There is no god but I, there is no god but I," which is also found in the Qur'ān. A person would certainly find it strange to hear his brother saying, "There is no god but I." He might think that this person is claiming divinity for himself, but it is only the utterance of the Real on his brother's tongue. And this brother himself hears the utterance of Allāh just as you might hear it coming from him, but he is not the speaker. Allāh spoke in this way to Moses with the tongue of the tree: "*Surely I am Allāh.*"[98] If He is capable of speaking

95 Qur'ān, 2:255.
96 Qur'ān, 1:5-6.
97 Qur'ān, 21:87.
98 Qur'ān, 20:14.

with the tongue of the tree by saying "Surely I am Allāh," He is also capable of using a human tongue to say, "Surely I am Allāh." If the servant has attained extinction, he knows there is nothing but Allāh.

There is found the sincere doctrine of Oneness (*tawḥīd*) that is demanded of the distinguished folk. Shaykh Aḥmad Tijānī said, as recorded in the *Jawāhir al-maʿānī*: "You have not perceived the reality of the doctrine of Unity as long as you say the creation and Allāh are both existing, for where is the Oneness if there are two? There is no oneness except when the oneness is for Allāh (alone), by Allāh (alone) and to Allāh (alone), and the servant does not enter in or exit from it." And the Shaykh said, "And this is not possible except through annihilation."

For this reason, the first thing the gnostics require of an aspirant is to find annihilation in Allāh the Blessed and Exalted. After that, the aspirant continues until he joins the Shaykh, for the Shaykh is the attribute (*ṣifa*) of Allāh. The goal of these two annihilations is that when the servant returns to a station (beyond annihilation) he will have already met with the Messenger of Allāh, may Allāh's peace and blessing be upon him, and with the Shaykh, for if he did not meet with them before his return, he will not know them afterward.[99]

When the aspirant passes through this, he returns to the witness of the created things, seeing their lack of existence and their existence at the same time. The semblance of that is the manner in which we view the cinema. If any of the gnostics among you has not yet seen the cinema, I would like that he see it, if only once. He will witness something and be certain that this nonexistent thing exists, as if what he sees is actually present. But in reality, of course, it does not exist. All of the

99 The "return" here seems to be a reference to the station of *baqāʾ*, or remaining in the world after the experience of *fanāʾ* (annihilation).

creation is like this, as (the images) in a cinema house only. You see something that is both present and non-existent.

With this knowledge you will be in the creation. You will do good deeds while knowing that you are in fact doing nothing, and you will avoid the bad while you are in fact not doing anything. The One is Allāh, the Blessed and Exalted, and He is the sole actor.

After this, the heart of the aspirant moves through the unseen worlds, (finding) nothing in them. Whether awake or asleep, he witnesses the unseen worlds, nothing in them. Then he becomes Divinely enraptured a second time, and returns again to Allāh the Blessed and Exalted. He knows for certain that there is nothing except Allāh – not by way of annihilation, spiritual intoxication, or rapture – but by perfect wakefulness. He knows there is nothing except Allāh. He becomes aware of things as they are (incumbent) upon him. So all the creation descends on his abode in which Allāh established him. But he knows there is nothing, and he gives dignity to things even though he does not consider them as existing. He is afraid of some things, though he does not consider them to exist. He loves things, though he does not consider them existing. Indeed, he undertakes all good works: he prays, he fasts, he makes pilgrimage, he gives in charity, and he spends of his wealth. All of this is for the sake of good conduct (*adab*) with Allāh the Blessed and Exalted, for he knows that nothing is there (except Allāh). Only when the servant arrives to this has he truly connected himself to Allāh. He does nothing except for the sake of Allāh, Blessed and Exalted is He. So long as the servant has not found this knowledge, perhaps he will perform actions thinking he is one doing them, and that while he is doing them his heart is present with Allāh. But he is not carrying out actions for the sake of Allāh the Blessed and Exalted. He is carrying out actions and performing good deeds, but not for the sake of Allāh's Countenance. He leaves aside bad things, but only because they will cause him to be blamed. This is not the (true) worship of Allāh. As the servant requires to become connected to Allāh the Blessed and Exalted with a firm bond, let his actions be pious deeds for the sake of Allāh the Blessed and Exalted, whether they are (bad things) abandoned or (good deeds) performed.

Everything belongs to Allāh the Blessed and Exalted. So the Qur᾽ān says, "*They were not commanded with anything except to worship Allāh, being completely sincere to Him in the religion.*"[100] Allāh commanded us to worship Him, and everything has the condition of sincerity (*ikhlāṣ*). Sincerity is the expulsion of equal partners in the affairs of the Real, the Blessed and Exalted. You yourself are an equal partner so long as there is a self (*nafs*). Expel the self from this work, and let the work be by Allāh, for Allāh, and to Allāh the Blessed and Exalted.

The Qur᾽ān says, "*You alone we worship, and You alone we ask for help.*"[101] "You alone we worship" is the station of the common folk. "You alone we ask for help" is the station of the elite. And the elite of the elite say nothing. The ritual prayer (*ṣalāt*) is the strongest of all bonds connecting the servant to Allāh the Blessed and Exalted. You must reflect on the ritual prayer. The entirety of the prayer is a pious deed and an adoration for the sake of Allāh the Blessed and Exalted. The best (of the prayer) is the reading of the Qur᾽ān, a continuous glorification in which there is nothing but contemplation. There is also the recitation itself, and the humility for the sake of Allāh the Blessed and Exalted in all movements and stillness (of the prayer). He said, "*I have not created the Jinn and the men except to worship Me.*"[102] In other words, "I have not created them for any other purpose except to worship Me alone." According to Ibn ʿAbbās,[103] the meaning (of "except to worship Me")

100 Qur᾽ān, 98:5.

101 Qur᾽ān, 1:5.

102 Qur᾽ān, 51:56.

103 The Prophet Muḥammad reportedly prayed for his companion Ibn ʿAbbās to attain special expertise in knowledge of the Qur᾽ān. He subse-

was "except to know Me" because if an action was performed by any except a gnostic (ʿārif), it might not be the worship of Allāh the Blessed and Exalted.

This is not the same as the children of Adam. If they should own slaves, the slaves will be divided into three groups depending on their purpose. One group performs different tasks to increase the owner's wealth. Another group is responsible for the preparation of food and drink in order to feed him. Another group, he asks to sit down, to leave off all that (other work), and to have the responsibility of being present with him. When he moves, they move with him. When he sits, they sit with him. Such are the people of proximity to Allāh the Blessed and Exalted. Allāh has denied having need of the first two groups of servants. "*I do not want provision from them, nor do I want them to feed Me.*"[104] He does not want that they should work for the sake of increasing His provision, as (human) masters want from their slaves. He does not want that they should work for Him for the sake of feeding Him or giving Him drink. Only the third group is left. These are the people of His love, those who are present with Him. They want their hands to be tied to His hands, they want to exalt Him, to glorify Him, to learn of His Majesty. They want nothing of the creation except to be of those who adore Him, those who are present with Him always.

Allāh the Blessed and Exalted created this creation and poured upon it His manifest and hidden blessing, from the first existence to this time of ours, and He has tended to them by sending them the Prophets calling to Allāh. When prophecy ended, the scholars (ʿulamāʾ) became the inheritors of the Prophets. The scholars have remained, calling to Allāh the Blessed and Exalted: all of them guide to Allāh.

---

quently became known as one of the best Qurʾān exegetes among the first generation of Muslims.

104 Qurʾān, 51:57.

Not all forms of love contain the guidance to Allāh the Blessed and Exalted. There may be deception among those who guide you to Allāh and who exhort you. Whoever points you toward the lower world (*dunyā*) has betrayed you. Whoever points you toward work has only exhausted you. The one who gives you sincere council is he who points you toward Allāh. The shaykh who is to be followed is he whose words guide you to Allāh the blessed and Exalted, and whose spiritual state (*ḥāl*) raises you to Allāh. And if you should perceive his state, your own spiritual aspiration (*himma*) is elevated toward Allāh. When he speaks, his words benefit you for the sake of Allāh because he speaks with wisdom (*ḥikma*).

The Blessed and Exalted said: "*And only a little of the knowledge has been made known to you.*"[105] "*And he to whom wisdom is granted has received abundant good.*"[106] Knowledge is rare, but wisdom is abundant. So what is wisdom? Wisdom is the knowledge taken directly from Allāh the Blessed and Exalted without any intermediary, but its possessor is not a Prophet. The Lord casts wisdom into the heart of His servant, and the servant receives it from his Lord directly. Then words proceed from Allāh that only pass through the speaker, and he is the first to benefit by them. These words appear from the Benefactor (*al-nāfiʿ*), who is Allāh, and Allāh is the sole Benefactor. As for words which appear from the corporal substance of man alone, they do not pass the ears, and they do not reach the heart, and few who listen to them benefit. If a speaker has been profuse with such words he may harden his heart by them. Such is not wisdom. It is from the favor and generosity of Allāh the Blessed and Exalted that, when Prophecy ceased, this inheritance (of wisdom) remained. This is what allows the servants to arrive to their Lord and connect themselves to Him, until Allāh inherits the earth and everything on it.

105 Qurʾān, 17:85.
106 Qurʾān, 2:269.

Allāh, sanctified and exalted is He, has gathered us in this moment, and in this blessed country. We implore Allāh to increase the blessing in this land.

(Now to return to) wisdom: when Allāh makes things for which He does not intend any benefit for His sake, He dresses them in frivolity. The works of Allāh are always so: whenever actions resemble frivolous vanity (*al-ʿabath*), such frivolity negates (the benefit of) their performance. Allāh said, "*Do they think that We have created them for (the pursuit of) frivolous vanity*?"[107] With this, Allāh is addressing the gnostics, those who witness that Allāh does not intend any benefit for Himself with His works. For us, doing things without benefit puts one in the domain of frivolity. Allāh does things without benefitting Himself, but He remains the Benefactor, even if His actions may (sometimes) appear fruitless. Wisdom (*al-ḥikma*) remains in such actions, for they were performed for the benefit of another. Wisdom is the performance of deeds for the benefit of someone other than oneself. This is why (in Arabic) a doctor is called a "wise one" (*ḥakīm*): all what the doctor does is for the benefit of others. Similarly, the actions of Allāh the sanctified and exalted are for the benefit of others.

So this one-time gathering, and subsequent parting, is not for the benefit of itself. It is for the benefit of some of us by others. The action thus becomes the (performance of) "wisdom", disassociated from frivolity and self-seeking. Indeed, we hope that in this gathering of ours, Allāh benefits all of us in this world and the next.

When Allāh wanted to increase something, He multiplied its (secondary) causes (*asbāb*), for if its causes should increase, the thing itself will increase. In this material world, we see two things that have many causes, so that everything to do with these things is multiplied. The causes for sustenance (*rizq*) in

107 Qurʾān, 23:115.

the world are plentiful. Everyone does something that causes him to obtain provision, and another person does something different that causes him to obtain a different provision. In this way, provision has become bountiful in this world. Death also has many causes. One person dies for one reason, and another dies for a different reason. Death is found by many means, so there is much death. We hear so-and-so died, and another so-and-so died, until we ourselves will die.

Forgiveness also has many causes. Indeed, we implore Allāh that it should have many causes. Indeed, there are many ways to obtain forgiveness mentioned in the sacred law. Among them is sitting with the righteous folk, or sitting for the remembrance (of Allāh), or (to hear) an exhortation. Indeed, with one sitting in a gathering of goodness, Allāh covers over two million (attendances at) gatherings of evil. May Allāh make our gathering and our parting a means for forgiving some of us by the means of others, and may He benefit some of us by the means of others of us.

I advise you, as in the beginning of this talk, with the fear (*taqwā*) of Allāh secretly and openly, and with the observance (*marāqaba*) of Him with each breath. It is by these two qualities that a person obtains what you have heard, and what you have not heard, concerning the people of goodness. These things cannot be obtained except by the fear of Allāh and the observance of Him. To be God-fearing is to implement the commands and to avoid the prohibitions. The observation of Allāh is to be engaged with Allāh at all times, as if he witnessed Allāh, as explained by the most truthful of speaker, "That is to worship Allāh as if you see Him, for if you do not see Him, He sees you." The individual thus worships Allāh, striving to be present to the majesty of Allāh, glorious and exalted, until it is as if he sees Him, even if he does not see Him. If a person does not arrive to this station, then he strives to be present to the intensity of Allāh's examination of every single part of the servant. Then he will know that, even if he does not see Allāh,

Allāh is always watching him. This is the lesser form of observation, but in both types there is blessing.

To worship Allāh as if you see him and as if He sees you is to know that Allāh is well acquainted (*muṭalliʿ*) with you in each moment of your lifespan. Whatever you do, and whatever you do not do, is witnessed by Allāh. Imagine you wanted to do a shameful act, but you knew that someone you consider a noble man was examining your every move. You would have to leave aside that act completely, whatever your desire, for you would hate that he should see you doing it. So you should reflect in everything that you want to do, for Allāh is well acquainted with you, how exalted is He! Allāh is indeed the greatest.

There was once a young slave girl who was one of the righteous. A man tried to entice her toward a shameful act. She said, "Alright, but only if it is in a place where no one can see us."

He said, "Yes!" And he closed all the doors to the house.

Then she said, "But two doors remain open. You must close them both before what you want can occur between us. There is one door by which Allāh sees us. As for me, so long as Allāh sees us, we can never do this shameful act. Moreover, there remains the fact that I see you, and that you see me. So if we were to do this act, you will know what I did, and I will know what you did. As long as these two doors remain open, I will never do this act."

In other words, a person must never commit an evil deed. There is no place that Allāh does not see him. "*There is not any affair in which you are engaged, whether reciting the Qurʾān or performing an action, except that We are witness to it.*"[108] Allāh perceives the servant with His knowledge, so that the knowledge (of his being perceived) is sufficient (to restrain him).

108 Qurʾān, 12:61.

However, the reality is that Allāh is present in His Essential Being (*dhāt*), with every creation in His Essence.

I was speaking to one jurist (*faqīh*), who said to me, "Your Shaykh al-Tijānī spoke about the present company (*ma'īya*) of Allāh's Essential Being (*dhāt*), but that is not possible."

I said to him, "Then what is this with us, if it is not Allāh with us in His Essential Being (*bi-dhātihi*): what is it that is with us?"

He told me, "It is the effects of His power."

I said, "This is the effects of power, yes truly, the effects of His power. But where did He go, Himself, for surely He has not changed His location? You and I cannot affect something in one place, and then go from that place. Allāh, according to the theology of the jurists (*fuqahā'*) cannot change locations. And since He has effected this (world), where has He gone?"

I said, "You jurists declare Allāh to be apart from His creation, and you say that the Essential Being of Allāh cannot be in a place that is dirty or impure. The unclean place is not befitting for His Essential Being, so you place Him outside this place. I say that if your aim had not been the (noble) declaration of Allāh's transcendence (*tanzīh*), you all would have entered the Hellfire. But still, you have made Allāh isolated and incapacitated from one place to another. This is impossible for His Reality, Blessed and Exalted is He."

I said to him, "Now, this very moment in which we are now has been brought forth in existence, created by Allāh the Blessed and Exalted. This very minute that they say we are living in now has been brought forth in existence, engendered by Allāh. This minute is with every creation in its essential being, whether in the East or West, in the heavens or on earth. Each and every creation is with this minute right now, and Allāh created this moment. The One who is capable of creating this moment and giving it the ability to be with each one of the creations in its very being; is this One unable to also be present with every single thing?"

He said to me, "You have healed my faith."

I said to him, "I also say to you that the Messenger of Allāh is with every single thing in his very person (*bi-dhātihi*)."

He said to me, "This is going beyond what you said before."

I said to him, "Do you pray?"

He said, "Yes!"

"Do you bear witness that there is no god except Allāh and that Muḥammad is His Messenger in the sitting position when you pray?"

"Yes," he said.

I said, "And when you read this testimony, do you not also say, 'Salutations of goodness and purity, may the peace and mercy of Allāh be upon you, O Prophet'[109]? The expression, 'upon you' (ʿalayk), can it be used in the Arabic language to address someone who is not present?"

"No," he said.

"So this Prophet," I said, "must be present with every one performing the ritual prayer from the East to the West?"

He said, "Yes."

Then I related the statement of the Prophet in Bukhārī,[110] "When someone dies, two Angels come to him (in the grave).

---

109 Along with the declaration of faith, this statement is a standard address every Muslim makes during his or her ritual prayer.

110 Bukhārī is the largest of the six canonical collections of Prophetic statements (*ḥadīth*).

They sit next to him and ask him, 'What do you know of this man (the Prophet)?' And the Messenger of Allāh, Allāh's peace and blessing upon him, is there sitting with the dead man in his grave."

I said to him, "And those who die, they number in the thousands every moment, and in every grave is found the Messenger of Allāh, Allāh's peace and blessing upon him. For the two Angels ask the dead person, 'What do you know of this man?' while the Messenger of Allāh, the blessing and peace of Allāh upon him, is sitting with him in the grave."

Then I said to him, "If the Prophet is present with these thousands of people, who die every second, are you not aware that the Prophet is present with every created thing by his very person?"

"Indeed," he said.

So Allāh is with every thing in His Essential Being, and we should observe Him in our works, in our words, in our spiritual states, and in our intentions, since He is well informed of all of us. There is nothing we can do that is hidden from Allāh the Blessed and Exalted. Shiblī[111] used to say, "Shameful deeds are attributed to what the servant has done, for even if Allāh should forgive him, Allāh the Blessed and Exalted has still seen what we have done." And Shiblī used to say, "As for shameful deeds, even if they are forgiven, in any case, the servant has still been exposed in the presence of his Lord." So if you are honored and graced with forgiveness, what has happened has still happened.

The religion of Islam is made up of the ritual prayer, fasting, alms giving, and pilgrimage. Alms and pilgrimage are only incumbent on the one who has the means. The alms-tax is only incumbent on those with wealth. The pilgrimage is only

---

111 Abū Bakr al-Shiblī (d. 946) was a Sufi and jurist of the Mālikī who was born and raised in Baghdad. He was a companion of Junayd.

incumbent on those who have the ability to go. As for the ritual prayer and fasting, they are incumbent on every person of responsibility (*mukallif*), man or woman, free person or slave, from the time of maturity to death. They are not obviated by a spiritual state among the states. Guard your ritual prayer! Guard your ritual prayer! In this fast-paced time, you see many youth claiming Islam while being heedless of the ritual prayer. Whoever leaves the prayer has left Islam completely. Allāh the Blessed and Exalted has prescribed the prayer in congregation, in specific times, and has prescribed humility in it. He mentioned those who perform the ritual prayer in this manner as the inheritors of the highest Paradise (*firdaws*). And He mentioned those who make sport of the prayer: they are Abū Jahl[112] and those who follow him in abandoning the prayer: "*He does not give in charity nor pray.*"[113] Then he mentioned their evil end when they are asked, "*What led you to the Hellfire? They will say, 'We were not of those who prayed.'*"[114] So those who leave the ritual prayer are the people of the Fire. On the other hand, those who return to the prayer with its proper conditions and requisite humility and conduct are the people of highest Paradise (*janna al-firdaws*) if Allāh so wills. One of the Messenger's companions asked him how to be close to him, Allāh's blessing and peace upon him, in Paradise. He told him, "Help me by increasing your prostrations." If he wanted to dwell in Paradise with the Messenger, Allāh's blessing and peace upon him, he had to help himself with lots of prayer. The Messenger and the shaykhs cannot lift the need to pray from their followers, nor can they take on the responsibility (*yatakallifūn lahum*) for their entry into Paradise. The Messenger is not capable of that, but rather he leads his companions and followers from being distant to the presence of Allāh. He commands them with what Allāh has commanded them, and he prohibits them from what Allāh

112 Abu Jahl, "the father of ignorance," is reference to ʿAmrū b. Hishām (d. 624), one of the chief opponents of the early Muslims in Mecca.

113 Qurʾān, 75:31.

114 Qurʾān, 74:42-43.

has prohibited them. So whoever follows him, enacting what he commands and abandoning what he prohibits, is with him in Paradise, and whoever does not do this will not be with him. The Messenger said (to his own daughter), "O Fāṭima, daughter of Muḥammad, I can avail you nothing against Allāh. Ask from my worldly possessions what you will, but in the Afterlife, none of you will come to the Afterlife except by the good deeds you have done. People will come to me by their deeds and their kindred relationships. And you will come to me by your kinship to the Messenger of Allāh, Allāh's peace and blessing upon him. But I can avail you nothing against Allāh (so come to me on account of your deeds). Thus I have conveyed the message."[115]

The Prophet guides humanity, but he is incapable of creating guidance himself. Rather, he points them to the path of guidance. The guide in reality is Allāh. The Messenger, the scholar, and the shaykh have nothing except guidance. They direct the aspirant to the path to the Afterlife. Whoever follows their example is felicitous with them, and whoever does not follow them, that is upon himself.

Our path is the Tijāniyya Sufi path, just as our religion is prayer and fasting. So our path is asking for forgiveness (*istighfār*), invoking blessings on the Prophet, may Allāh's blessing and peace be upon him, and (saying) "there is no god except Allāh." Many among the Muslims in this time are committing an astounding retrogression, until they become preoccupied with abandoning the prayer and the fast (of Ramadan), and with complete denial of the masters of the Sufi paths. The Sufi path (*ṭarīqa*) is nothing but the path of the Messenger of Allāh, Allāh's peace and blessing upon him. It does not belong to ʿAbd al-Qādir al-Jīlānī or to Shaykh Aḥmad al-Tijānī, may Allāh be pleased with them both. The Sufi path is acquired from the path of Allāh's Messenger, Allāh's blessing and peace upon

115 This narration in the Ḥadīth collection of Muslim was a result of the revelation of the verse, "And warn your nearest kindred" (Qurʾān, 26:214).

him, so it commands people with this acquisition so that they may derive benefit. Asking for forgiveness, invoking blessing on the Prophet, Allāh's blessing and peace upon him, and (saying) "there is no god except Allāh," are all things commanded by Allāh in His mighty book.

A scholar in Mecca advised me that I should command my followers to give up the Tijāniyya Sufi path, because it constituted innovation, superstition, and unbelief (*kufr*). He said, "Your conformity (to Islamic principles) has been favorably received, and we know that you are a scholar. (In order to effect our design) we would only need that you take up the responsibility of returning to your country and expelling people from the Tijāniyya Sufi path."

"Yes," I told him, "speak, say what you want to say." So he spoke until he had finished his words. Then I asked him, "What is the Tijāniyya Sufi path?"

He told me. "I don't know."

I said, "You are right that you don't know. I know the Tijāniyya Sufi path, and I know Shaykh al-Tijānī, may Allāh be pleased with him. I know them both very well, but you do not know either of them. Is it you who should teach me, or I who should teach you?"

He said to me, "Yes, who knows a thing, it is he who should teach it."

So I said to him, "Now, you have asked about the Tijāniyya Sufi path, and you are not teaching me about the Tijāniyya. The Tijāniyya is asking for forgiveness from Allāh, invoking blessing on the Prophet, and saying 'there is no god except Allāh.' Allāh says, 'Seek forgiveness from your Lord.'[116] And who is free from sin? The Prophet, Allāh's blessing and peace upon him, was so safeguarded, since Allāh forgave his previous and

116 Qur'ān, 71:10.

future sins. But even he said, 'I ask Allāh for forgiveness seventy times a day.' In another narration, he said, 'one hundred times a day.' So even the one who has been safeguarded from was unable to abandon seeking forgiveness. As for myself and you, surely we must seek forgiveness."

"Yes," he said.

"As for invoking blessing and peace on the Prophet, Allāh's peace and blessing upon him, Allāh said, 'invoke blessings (all of you) on him, and offer him greetings of peace.'[117] The noble Messenger said, 'Whoever offers one prayer on me, Allāh offers ten prayers on him.' Can a Muslim advise another Muslim to abandon that?"

"No," he said.

I said to him, "And can a Muslim advise another Muslim to stop saying 'there is no god except Allāh'?"

"No," he said.

I said, "This is the Tijāniyya Sufi path: asking forgiveness, invoking blessings on the Prophet, Allāh's blessing and peace upon him, and saying 'there is no god except Allāh.' This is recited morning and evening. If you say this is an innovation, know that innovation is something that does not come in the Qur᾽ān or in the sayings of the Prophet. Our litany (*wird*) is first made up of seeking refuge in Allāh from the accursed Satan, then reciting the opening chapter of the Qur᾽ān (*fātiḥa al-kitāb*). Allāh said, '*So recite of it (the Qur᾽ān) what is easy for you.*'[118] Then, asking for forgiveness: '*Ask forgiveness of your Lord, for indeed He is oft-forgiving.*'[119] Then the invocation of blessing on the Prophet: '*Invoke blessings (all of you) on him,*

117 Qur᾽ān, 33:56.
118 Qur᾽ān, 73:20.
119 Qur᾽ān, 71:10.

and offer him greetings of peace.'[120] Then saying, 'there is no god except Allāh.' Allāh said, '*And remember Allāh with bountiful remembrance.*'[121] The only remaining particularity is the performance of the litany in the morning and in the evening. Allāh said, '*Glorify Him in the morning and evening.*'[122] And He said, '*In the mornings and late afternoons.*'[123] All of this is in the Qur᾽ān. Would you bid me to abandon this?"

He said, "No. But you should write a book in which you clarify for me what the Tijāniyya Sufi path actually is, so that we may know what is valid from that which is invalid."

I told him, "Sure, the Tijāniyya Sufi path is this: asking forgiveness from Allāh, invoking blessings on the Prophet – the door to Allāh the Blessed and Exalted – and saying 'there is no god except Allāh.'"

The goal is the remembrance of Allāh, and the statement "there is no god except Allāh" has two meanings, as I said earlier. It has a shell and core, and a core of the core. "There is no god except Allāh:" there is nothing worshipped alongside the Real, except Him. This is the station of the common folk. As for the meaning of "there is no god except Allāh" among those aspiring, it is that there is no purpose alongside the Real, except Allāh. As for the meaning of "there is no god except Allāh" among those arrived: there is nothing that exists with the Real, except Allāh.

First there is the companion of "there is no god but Him." Second there is the companion of "there is no god but You." Third there is the companion of "there is no god but I." This is

120 Qur᾽ān, 33:56.

121 Qur᾽ān, 33:41.

122 Qur᾽ān, 33:42.

123 Qur᾽ān, 24:36. This verse refers to times when Allāh's name is commemorated in the "houses (mosques or retreats) that Allāh has authorized to be raised."

how Allāh is remembered, "*Allāh, Allāh,*" just as I hear you all saying.

Thus, the remembrance of Allāh the Blessed and Exalted is the key to sainthood. The remembrance is the beginning of sainthood; indeed, it is the beginning and end of sainthood. Always, the remembrance is found in the beginning, and the remembrance is found in the end. The end is always in the beginning. Where there is the beginning there is the end. If you perfect the beginning, you have perfected the end. We have begun first of all with "there is no god except Allāh," then, "there is no god but You," then, "there is no god but I." Allāh, to Him you are all returning. And you should all say, "there is no god but Allāh, the Blessed and Exalted."

Africa for the Africans

Shaykh Ibrāhīm Niasse wrote "Africa for the Africans"[124] in response to the Archbishop of Dakar, Marcel Lefebvre,[125] who wrote a series of polemical articles equating Islam with "Communist" oppression in the late 1950s. Noted historian Vincent Monteil summarized Lefebvre's stance with the following citations from the Archbishop:[126]

---

124 The Arabic text can be found in Niasse, *Saʿādat al-anām bi-aqwāl shaykh al-islām* (Edited Shaykh al-Tijānī b. ʿAlī Cissé, Cairo: al-Sharika al-Dawliyya, 2006), 65-68. Amar Samb included a French translation of the work in *Essai sur al contribution du Sénégal à la Littérature d'Expression Arabe* (Dakar: IFAN, 1972), 223-226.

125 Lefebvre served as Dakar's Archbishop, responsible for the whole of West Africa and a Catholic population of roughly 50,000, from 1947-1962. He was known for his conservative opinions and his opposition to the second Vatican council after his return to France in 1962. In 1976, Pope Paul VI censured him for ordaining priests without the permission of the Vatican. When he consecrated a bishop in 1988 without Vatican approval, Pope John Paul II had him excommunicated. Lefebvre died of cancer in 1991. See Bernard Tissier de Mallerais, *Marcel Lefebvre, the Biography* (Kansas City, Missouri: Angelus Press, 2004).

126 See Vincent Monteil, *Islam Noir: une religion à la conquête de l'Afrique* (Paris, 1964), 194-195. See also Samb, *Contribution du Sénégal*, 223-226.

Either Africa will follow its profound aspirations of simplicity, honesty and religion; and it will become Catholic; or, without religion, it will become confirmed in its vices of polygamy, of domination of the weak and of superstition; and abandon itself to Islam.[127]

Lefebvre finally provoked the response of Niasse with a later article of the Archbishop that tried to link Islam to Communism, and thus to ensure the West's castigation of Islam in the emerging post-colonial order. Lefebvre wrote in 1959:

The stranglehold of Russia and China on Africa everyday becomes more of a reality! This is not surprising for those who understand Islam: the countries with majority Muslim population are those that detach themselves most quickly from the West, calling for communistic methods similar to those of Islam: fanaticism, collectivism, slavery of the weak. All of this is in keeping with Islam.[128]

Niasse's response came three weeks later and was published in Arabic by Times Press Lagos (Nigeria).[129] Mervyn Hiskett, the first historian to analyze the work, believed it was "essentially a claim that Africa could find unity through Islam," thus a coherent tract of Islamic pan-Africanism.[130] Rüdiger Seesemann disagreed, describing the piece more as an "immediate and direct response to Lefebvre" rather than a treatise on African nationalism.[131] While Lefebvre's diatribes were obviously

---

127 According to Monteil and Samb, this article appeared in *Ecclésia,* 46, January, 1953.

128 According to Monteil and Samb, this article appeared in *France Catholique*, December 18, 1959.

129 Niasse, "Ifrīqiyya ilā l-Ifrīqiyyīn", *Times Press Lagos,* January 5, 1960.

130 Mervyn Hiskett, "The Community of Grace and its Opponents, the Rejectors: a debate about theology and mysticism in Muslim West Africa with special reference to its Hausa expression," in *African Language Studies*, 17 (1980), 108-109.

131 Rüdiger Seesemann, *Nach der Flut: Ibrāhīm Niasse (1900-1975), Su-*

the immediate context, "Africa for the Africans" has had a wide appeal in Senegal, Nigeria, Ghana, America and other places with substantial African or African diaspora Muslim populations. The work has certainly contributed to the image of Niasse as a prominent Muslim pan-African intellectual.

* * *

In each tribe, there is the Banū Saʿd.[132] Thus did I learn of a surprising address written by Lefebvre, the Archbishop of Dakar, and published in the journal, *La France Catholique*, in December, 1959, commemorating the revered birth (of Jesus); an address which tarnished the honor of Islam, the honor of our homeland (*waṭan*), and by this latter I mean black Africa. I have examined closely certain of his passages, and found them motivated by bigotry and injustice.

I begin responding to these passages by recalling a few verses from the Wise Remembrance (the Qurʾān), the constitution of the Islamic community (*milla*), (a revelation) into which error cannot enter, whether from front or behind, "*a revelation from (Allāh) the Wise, the Praiseworthy.*"[133]

"*Say, O Allāh, the possessor of sovereignty! You give power to whom You will and You remove from power whom You will, and You exalt whom You will and You debase whom You will. All good lies in Your hands, and You have power over all things.*"[134]

---

fik und Gesellschaft in Westafrika (PhD thesis, University of Beyrouth, 2004), 688-689.

132 Proverb signifying, according to Amar Samb's French notation, that "each tribe has its defender, and here each religion has its defender or each continent has its advocate."

133 Qurʾān, 41:42.

134 Qurʾān, 3:25.

"Surely the earth belongs to Allāh, and He bequeaths it to whom He wills among His servants, and the (good) end is for the righteous."135

"Among His signs are the night, the day, the sun and the moon; do not prostrate to the sun or to the moon; prostrate to Allāh who created them if it is truly Him you worship."136

"Say: He is Allāh, the Unique

Allāh the Eternal Absolute

He did not beget, nor is He begotten of

And there is nothing comparable to Him."137

By the first verse mankind realizes that sovereignty belongs to Allāh, in Africa as elsewhere. He entrusts with power whomever He wills and He deposes whomever He wills. The second verse adds that the successful end is only for the righteous. With the third, everything besides Allāh is rejected (as an object of worship), whether the stars, the moon, or, more explicitly, the Christian cross. The last verses indicate that the Most High is One, Singular, Unique, the Eternal Absolute; He does not have children nor was He born, and there is nothing comparable to Him. Thus does mankind realize that the exalted Originator is the Benefactor for Africa and elsewhere, and He provides health and well-being. Every homeland (*waṭan*) has a people (*qawm*), and every people a homeland. We are the people of Africa, so Africa belongs to us, and we belong to Africa. Sooner or later every nation (*waṭan*) will come to be governed by its children whatever the schemes of the enemies of the African citizenry (*jinsiyya*).

A current of freedom and nationalism has burst forth in this twentieth century, and nothing can stop it. Every land will

---

135 Qurʾān, 7:125.

136 Qurʾān, 41:37.

137 Qurʾān, 112:1-4.

come to be governed by its people, whether they are Muslim, Christian, or Communists, since the people are stronger than the governments. In any case, the rule of the foreigner in a foreign land has passed, never to return. Therefore: Africa belongs to the Africans!

Seizing power is one thing, but religious adherence is another. If we return to the religious question, this is the declaration of the Qurʾān, the last revelation from Allāh: "*Surely the religion in the presence of Allāh is submission* (*al-Islām*)."[138] And who does not believe in the declaration of the Qurʾān, does not believe in Allāh alone as we have presented. He believes in something that cannot hear, cannot see; an inanimate object that was created by Allāh or manufactured by man himself; such as the Christian cross or images incarnate. Allāh is greater (than what they imagine)!

Who desires to do justice must know men by the Truth, and not the Truth by men.[139] In all religions there are those who are ideal exemplars and those who are flawed. If you should encounter the faults of some Muslims in their Islam, this is an injustice and a transgression (of the religion), an oppression and an outrage.

But it is a great lie to say that Communism is found wherever Islam in found. Communism has mostly spread in lands that have not yet become attached to Islam. The truth is that Islam opposes Communism, as Communism opposes Islam. Indeed, was the appearance of Communism in Europe the result of Islam? Certainly not! Communism did not emerge in Africa, and where it has appeared, it is only on those lands whose people are not Muslims. Islam entered this land of ours, even if its origins were from elsewhere, centuries before the arrival of Europeans. Neither Communism nor Christianity

138 Qurʾān, 3:19.

139 Saying generally attributed first to ʿAlī b. Abī Ṭālib, the son-in-law of the Prophet Muḥammad and the fourth Caliph after him.

entered our lands except after Europeans seized power here. Therefore, the presence of Communism will not materialize with the liberation of the country from foreign rule. Rather, the contrary is the case.

As for the alleged servitude of mankind (under Islam), let us ask ourselves: was it not a few European Christians who invaded Africa and colonized it, and was it not they who tried to enslave people? Or was it the Muslims? As for the propensity of some groups of mankind to enslave other groups, the Qur᾿ān — the constitution of Islam — has this to say: "*O people of the Book! Let us come to an understanding between us and you: that we worship none but Allāh and that we do not associate anything with Him, and that some of us do not take others as masters in the place of Allāh.*"[140]

When children of a certain class retain certain prerogatives, whether kings or clergy, this can be called subjugation of the people. Surely the prerogatives of kings, governments, and religions as they exist outside of Africa and among non-Muslims, are a greater and more severe danger to the powerless and the working class (than such privileges in Muslim Africa).

A Christian writer posed the question: "Has real equality been attained in the West, even after the French Revolution and the declaration of human rights?" Then he asked, "Have not the prerogatives of the kings, nobles, the holders of rank and titles and the men of religion persisted, and have not the children of kings and nobles retained preferences in full presence of the common law? Have not such people contrived for themselves, in the face of the common law, privileges other than those designated for the commoners and the needy? Such people pay neither duties nor taxes." Then he said, "Do you not perceive that these Western states privilege a large group of religious men, who own a third of the country's land and a third

140 Qur᾿ān, 3:57.

of the nation's real estate? Their land is exempt from property taxes; they are except from customs taxes. Their revenues multiply, their trade increases and they become hoarders of gold." This is what the Christian writer himself said.

This is the subjugation of the people. The workers, the indigent, and the suffering peasants pay the rising taxes while the lazy, idle priests become abundantly rich, until each one has more than one thousand commoners have altogether. And all of this is alongside the call for justice, fair treatment, and equality. Surely there is a great difference between this and the (Islamic) obligation of almsgiving (*zakat*) on the rich, restored directly to the poor.

As for the education, instruction, and culture provided by the Christian missionaries, as the writer (Lefebvre) claims, it amounts to only ten percent of the education provided by the scholars of Islam in the farthest reaches of Africa. The truth is that there is no learning except their learning, no instruction except their instruction, and no culture except their culture. (Even now) are not the number of mosques, gathering places, and schools — in which they have always volunteered their learning — multiple times the number of churches (and missionary schools)? In all of this, there is no government support: the Muslims have always depended on Allāh and themselves. Moreover, these schools demonstrate equality and the observance of human rights, which is more than can be said in the non-Muslim schools.

The writer (Lefebvre) shamelessly declared, "The blindest adherence to tradition, the most mindless subjection, and the enslavement of the weak: these are the traditions of Islam."

(O Lefebvre!) Your love of something can be a veil to its ugliness, and your hatred of another things can be a veil to its beauty. The writer (Lefebvre) has thus described Islam with the attributes of his own religion, for only they (the Christians) say that religion is external to reason (ʿaql), relishing between themselves the people's submission to them. They do not search for the truths in their religion, rather they practice blind adherence to tradition and mindless subjection.

If a people should accuse me, I return the accusation to them.

In this, am I unjust to the people of Hamdan?[141]

If you return (to this argument), we will also return, for the injustice lies with him who began (this fight). The rest of his clumsy jabs do not merit response. "*Peace is on him who follows guidance, and retribution is on him who gives lie to the truth and turns away.*"[142]

---

141 This could be a reference to the powerful tribe, the Banū Hamdān, of pre-Islamic Yemen, who resisted initial calls to Islam from the Prophet Muḥammad, who sent Khālid b. al-Walīd to convert the Yemenis.

142 Qurʾān, 20:50.

Chapter II

Public Wolof-language Speeches in Senegal

The Eternal Islam

Shaykh Ibrāhīm delivered this speech for the celebration of the Prophet's birthday (mawlid) in Medina-Kaolack, Senegal on July 19, 1965. An English version of the speech first appeared in a July 25, 1992 edition of Al Faydatou Tijania magazine (Cairo: Muḥammad Ma'mun Niasse). The speech was originally delivered in Wolof, although the name of the translator(s) is not given. However, those undertaking the issue's redaction (and thus matters of translation) include: Bachir Niasse, Babacar Seck, Ali Sokhna, Ali Biteye, Sidi Arabi Niasse, Ibrāhīm Thiam, Ibrāhīm Sall, Boubacar Thiam, and Arab Diop. A slightly different edited version appeared in Abdul Hakim Halim (ed.), Shaykh al Islam al Ḥājj Ibrāhīm Niasse, Ṭarīqa Tijaniyya: selected writings about Shaykh Ibrāhīm Niasse (Detroit: African American Islamic Institute, 2000), p. 19-26. The version below represents further editing for coherency, with the permission of Shaykh Ḥasan Cissé given in 2006.

* * *

Praise be to Allāh, who has honored and favored us by sending our master Muḥammad to us. Allāh's prayer and peace is upon him, now as it was with the previous generations. On his account, Allāh said, "*And We have not sent you (O Muḥammad) except as a mercy to all the worlds.*"[143] Through him, Allāh gave us the gift of His revelation, His clear path for those striving for righteousness. With him, Allāh has sent the religion of truth, "*so that He may exalt it above all religions.*"[144]

May the peace and blessings of Allāh be upon him, his family, his virtuous companions, and all those who follow him until the Day of Judgment.

On this occasion of the *mawlid* – the remembrance of the birth of light itself, the eye of bountiful deliverance in this world and the next – let us renew our attachment to the faith of Islam, the everlasting religion of Allāh. Indeed, Allāh's satisfaction lies in our refusal of anything other than Islam. As in the Qur᾿ān, "*He who follows another religion besides Islam, his religion will not be accepted of him.*"[145]

Islam is the belief in One God. The resignation to the Will of Allāh is the realization of justice among people. The Qur᾿ān reveals that all of the Prophets of Allāh have used the same word to describe their religion: al-Islam or "submission." Islam is surely the universal religion, encompassing all the other religions. The stains of man cannot obscure or modify its essential beauty. Islam was the belief and method of worship prescribed for Abraham, Moses, and Jesus Christ. Its meaning has not changed: release yourself into the worship of Allāh and do not divide yourselves to its purpose.[146] As for those religions

143 Qur᾿ān, 21:107.

144 Qur᾿ān, 61:9.

145 Qur᾿ān, 3:85.

146 The Shaykh is likely referring to the verse: "*He has ordained for you the same way of religion which He had enjoined on Noah, and that We have now revealed to you (O Muḥammad), and which We had already enjoined*

the Qur᾿ān mentions as having been altered by later followers, they had already become irreparably distant from the essential truth of Islam before becoming nullified by successive revelations. The last revelation, which abrogates the previous revelations, is the religion of Muḥammad. "*This community of yours is one community, and I am your Lord, so worship Me*!"[147]

This is the refuge we are offering to the whole world – Africans, Europeans, Asians, Americans – "*Let us come to an understanding between us and you, that we should not worship anything apart from Allāh, and that we ascribe no partners to Him and take no other protector besides Him. If they turn their backs on this, tell them: 'Bear witness that we have submitted to Allāh as Muslims.'*"[148]

Islam's doctrine is simple, and its principals are not limited by a particular time or place. Indeed, there is nothing worthy of worship apart from Allāh. Muḥammad, Allāh's peace and blessings upon him, is Allāh's servant and messenger. All human beings are equal: there is no privilege for the white man over the red, yellow, or black man except by righteousness (*taqwā*). Righteousness, as the Qur᾿ān says, is simply to obey the commands of Allāh and to avoid His prohibitions.

Islam emphasizes the importance of the family, for its rights are inextricably bound to the society and world at large. Islam has clarified for us all social relations, from the individual's duty to himself to his duty to his family, society, and government.

Incumbent on each individual, whether man or woman, is good conduct and manners (ādāb). The Prophet said, "The most perfect of believers is the most perfect in manners." Allāh Himself praised His Prophet by saying, "*Surely you have the*

---

on Abraham and Moses and Jesus, saying: 'Establish the Religion and be not divided in it'" (Qur᾿ān, 42:13).

147 Qur᾿ān, 21:92.

148 Qur᾿ān, 3:64.

most exalted of character."[149] And ʿĀʾisha said, "His character was the Qurʾān." His behavior is an example for other men and all creatures. A good Muslim strives to improve his character and to benefit his fellow man.

In Islam, the basis of familial relations is love and leniency. Allāh says, "*Among His signs is that He has created for you a pair from yourself, as source of tranquility, placing between you (husband and wife) love and leniency.*"[150] Allāh also said, "*Your wives are a garment for you, and you are a garment for them.*"[151] And He said, "Wives have rights the same as those invested in their husbands."[152] However, "*Men are the protectors of women.*"[153] This pre-eminence relates to men taking care of women and their administration of the family, a function indispensable in the family unit as with other associations.

Islam regards society as the reunification of members of the same body. For this reason, Muslims must be preoccupied with the welfare of the needy and the poor, providing them assistance through charitable endeavors. Allāh said: "*Provide assistance to each other, for the sake of righteousness and the awe of Allāh.*"[154]

In relation to authority, Allāh says, "*Their affairs are determined by mutual consultation.*"[155] Allāh sets the standard for those in authority with the example of the Prophet: "*With the grace of your Lord, you have been conciliatory and easy with them. If you had been rude or hard of heart, they would have detached themselves from you. So look past their faults and forgive them. Consult with them in matters, and when you have decided, seek the support of Allāh.*"[156]

---

149 Qurʾān, 68:4.
150 Qurʾān, 30:21.
151 Qurʾān, 2:187.
152 Qurʾān, 2:228.
153 Qurʾān, 4:34.
154 Qurʾān, 5:2.
155 Qurʾān, 42:38.
156 Qurʾān, 3:159.

Our Lord is One. We are all descendants of the same person: Adam. O Muslims of the East and the West: let us value this immense treasure. It contains all we need for peace, prosperity, and progress. There is no safety, salvation, or peace for one who does not attach himself to this single rope of Allāh. "*Hold to the rope of Allāh in unity, and be not divided among yourselves.*"[157] And the best of advice comes from him who has first followed his own advice, for it is impossible to instruct others before first instructing oneself.

O People of Islam! Those of us who have left the principals of our religion to ape the customs of non-Muslims have met with ruin. Materialism can only feed the ego, not the spirit; and without the spirituality of Islam, there is only devastation. In this time especially, let those who believe make their hearts humble before Allāh and grateful for the truth He has sent down. Let us not be like those who received the scriptures of old, but were impatient with the decree of Allāh, and their hearts became hardened and corrupt.

The Muslim community flourished in the beginning of its history because it followed the prescriptions of the Holy Qur᾽ān. And Allāh does not change the state of a people until they change their own internal condition.[158] If we are to protect ourselves from the manifest threats to our communities looming on the horizon, we must revisit our past methods. Let us be united under the banner of mercy and benevolence to attain the security of the two abodes.

The call to Islam, by giving sincere advice and discouraging ugliness and injustice, is obligatory on Muslim preachers. And what a blessing it is for such preachers to emerge from an entire community of Muslims calling to goodness, cooperating in righteousness and benevolence, and prohibiting injustice and transgression.

157 Qur᾽ān, 1:103.

158 A variation of the Qur᾽ān verse, 13:11.

In a Ḥadīth related by ʿAlī, the Prophet said, "What would become of you if your daughters should become spoiled and your wives debauched?" His followers asked, "O Messenger of Allāh! How could that happen?" The Prophet said, "This and much more will befall you if you allow the blameworthy to become virtuous and the virtuous to become blameworthy."

It is reported by Abū Dāwūd and al-Tirmidhī that the Prophet was asked about the verse: "I recommend you to your purified selves." [159] The Prophet said, "Commend and assist one another with the good, and prohibit the bad. If avarice is obeyed and lust followed, the world will be turned upside down, and everyone will be amazed at what he will see. I recommend you to your purified selves."

It is obligatory to send Muslim missionaries to exemplify Islam to the non-Muslims. For those who say such is contrary to Islam, consider the Ḥadīth of ʿAmrū b. al-ʿĀṣ in al-Ṭabarānī. The Prophet said, "Similar to Jesus sending out his apostles, I am sending out Muʿādh b. Jabal, Sālim Abū Hudhayfa, Ibn Mahbir and Ibn Masʿūd." A man said, "Are not Abū Bakr and ʿUmar better suited as missionaries?" The Prophet answered: "But I cannot do without them, their place with me is as the sight and hearing to the human body."

Muslims, particularly the scholars, must take up this mission to call all human beings to what will benefit them. For indeed, a day is coming when fortune and children will not benefit a person, and only he who comes before Allāh with a clean heart will be saved.[160]

---

159 A reference to the verse of the Qurʾān (5:105), "*O you who believe! Guard your souls*" (ʿalaykum anfusakum), about which Abū Bakr al-Ṣaddīq similarly reported the Prophet's explanation, "When the people see a wrong-doer committing a wrong and do not seize his hand to restrain him, it is most likely that Allāh would inflict them with His chastisement" (in Abū Dāwūd, Tirmidhī and Nisāʾī; contained in *Riyad al-Salihin*, chapter 24, Ḥadīth 199).

160 Variation of the Qurʾān verse, 26:88-89.

Rulers of the Muslim world must do their best to realize the unity of the believers, both in speech and action. The ranks of the Muslims must not exclude anyone on the basis of race or skin-color. To be related through religion is above all other relationships. Islam condemns all racial and tribal divisions.

I invite all the rulers of the world exercising authority over Muslims, whether they themselves are Muslim or non-Muslim, to avoid implementing measures in contradiction with the Noble Qur᾽ān. Muslims will never support an action undermining the honor of Islam. These rulers must enact severe penalties for those practicing usury. Allāh has made commerce lawful but has prohibited usury, warning that He will nullify its gains and multiply the fruits of charity.[161] Usury holds no benefit in the next life, nor does it provide any benefit to the economies of nations here and now.

O Muslims! Many people in Africa and Asia have become newly independent from colonial domination. But national sovereignty does not guarantee them any stability. Oppression and injustice still infect their societies, without Muslims being able to escape. Some Muslims have been so nauseated by the situation that they have even preferred to be ruled by non-Muslim governments. However, the inequality and injustice against which they are revolting cannot be ascribed to Islam itself, but only to reactionary leaders far from the true principals of their religion.

I pray that Allāh preserve the Muslims from the misdeeds of the unjust. The Prophet, as reported in Bukhārī, said, "There are three types of injustice: that which is never forgiven by Allāh, that which can be pardoned by Allāh, and that which Allāh never fails to redress." The injustice that is never forgiven is *shirk*, or associating partners with Allāh. The injustice that Allāh may pardon is that committed by servants against

161 Qur᾽ān, 2:276.

themselves in leaving the prescriptions of Allāh. The injustice that Allāh never fails to redress is that committed against one's fellow human being.

Beware of injustice, for if it persists, it can only bring destruction. A believer can live for a long time with those of no faith, but he will not last long with the unjust. Many of today's leaders manipulate every means at their disposal for unjust purposes.

I cannot end this talk without reciting a relevant passage from the Qur'ān, the Book which is sufficient as a constitution for the entire world: "*Follow the straight path as has been ordained on you. Do not follow the vain doctrines of those without faith. Say, I believe in the scripture that has been sent down. He has ordered me to deal fairly with you. Allāh is our Lord and your Lord, the recompense of our deeds is for us, and the recompense of your deeds is for you. Let there be no argument between us and you: Allāh will decide between us, and to Him we are returning.*"[162] The meaning of these verses is clear, no person or society can misunderstand them.

I am proud, on these days of celebration for the Muslim world, to gather with all Muslims, including my Arab Muslim brothers here. The ethnic diversity at our celebrations should not be surprising because we are all brothers through Islam: our actions are related, and our hopes and sufferings are one. My hopes for salvation for myself and for you all are with Allāh.

I conclude with a prayer to Allāh the Most High, that He reform, assist, and raise up the people of Muḥammad, wherever they may be throughout the world, until they become exalted through governing themselves by what Allāh has revealed. May Allāh grant you prosperity in this life and the next, and may we all attain His salvation and benediction.

---

162 Qur'ān, 42:15.

The Heritage of the Prophet

(Speech for the Mawlid)

The following two speeches are excerpted from the "Mine of Wisdom," a 1989 collection of particularly famous Wolof speeches of Shaykh Ibrāhīm Niasse in Medina-Kaolack, Senegal, in the late 1960s and early 1970s. The 1989 English translation of these speeches, by Abdur Rahman Aḥmad of the Zawiya Erubu in Ilorin, Nigeria, bore the full title, *Mine of Wisdom: Selected speeches of Maulana Sheikh Ibrāhīm Niasse* (Lagos: al-Tawheed Publishing). The cover says the work was translated by Shaykh Ali Cissé, but likely this means Shaykh Ali translated the speech's contents into Hausa for a Nigerian audience, who later provided an English translation (Shaykh Ali did not speak English). This first English version was later reprinted in its original by Abdul Halim Hakim (Detroit: African American Islamic Institute, 2001).

As recordings of the Shaykh's speeches still exist, the assistance of Mouhamadou Mahi Thiam has been indispensable in reorganizing and editing this text based on the original Wolof. Speech titles are my own creation, inserted to simply give the reader some idea of the contents that follow. In most cases, customary greetings and the welcoming of various dignitaries have been omitted. Readers familiar with the speeches in their original Wolof will also notice the omission of certain passages, due to their absence in the original English versions. For these reasons, these selections cannot claim to be more than excerpts from the original speeches.

* * *

There once lived a saint of Allāh who claimed that his kingdom was greater than the Kingdom of Allāh. Those who heard him were baffled. He said, "It is no blasphemy, as the Prophet himself said, 'If you are for Allāh, Allāh will be for you.' Bear witness that Allāh, Who is All-Powerful and Exalted above His creation, is certainly greater than His kingdom."

Let us all live for Him; and He, the Oft-Forgiving, the Most Merciful, the Most Bountiful, the Bearer of the Highest Names, will be for us. What Allāh prefers most among all His creation is His servant who believes only in Him, that He alone is worthy of worship, that He bore no child, that He was not born Himself, that He has no resemblance of any kind, and that He does not associate partners with Himself.

He is the First, the only Existence before existence and the only Existence after creation ceases to exist. I often meditate on the ineffable and unfathomable cataclysm that will occur when all the innumerable manifestations of Allāh cease to exist and nothing is left but Allāh, the Last. Only Allāh existed in the beginning before creation, and only He will exist when the creation has ended; and there has never been a change in His Essence.[163]

---

163 Such an idea is reminiscent of the statement of ʿAlī b. Abī Ṭālib: "Surely, after the extinction of the world, Allāh the Glorified will remain alone with nothing beside Him. He will be, after its extinction, as He was before its production: without time or place or moment or period, and years and hours will disappear. There will be nothing except Allāh, the One, the

The creation came into existence only when His Spirit manifested into the light of Muḥammad. Out of this light Allāh made the rest of creation, both the material world and the Hereafter.

In *Ḥadīth Qudsī*, Allāh says, "If not for you (O Muḥammad), I would not have brought forth the creation. I created you for Myself and made the rest of creation for you." The Prophet said, "All Muslims are from my light and my light is from the light of Allāh." All of creation – believers and non-believers, the heavens and earth – came from his light and his light came from Allāh. How great a kingdom it is, without limit or frontier. All these are signs of Allāh, the Supreme Being, and manifestations of His sublime light.

We are all one, all the offspring of one man; we are all the children of one father – Adam. Allāh said that He created Adam in His image, and created the rest of the creation for his accommodation. If all the children of Adam should perish from the face of the earth, Allāh will fold up heaven and earth like a prayer mat, stopping the sun from rising and setting, removing the moon and stars, destroying day and night, eliminating the seasons – rain, sun, sleet, and snow. At this point the children of Adam will depart to their various stations in Paradise and Hell, where they will remain for eternity.

When the end arrives, nothing will exist except Allāh – the Most Merciful, the Most Bountiful – in complete and total solitude. All that we enjoyed up to this point will come to nothing, as it will no longer exist. The only manifestation will be

---

All-Powerful." In another sermon, Ali said, "He is the First for whom there was no 'before' so that there could be anything before Him. He is the Last for whom there is 'after' so that there could be anything after Him. Time does not change over Him, so as to admit of any change of condition about Him." (See Ali Reza (translated), *Peak of Eloquence, Nahjul Balagha: Sermons, Letters and Sayings of Imam Ali ibn Abu Talib* (New York: Tahrike Tarsile Qur'ān, 1996), 375, 222.

found in the Hereafter, where mankind will remain until the cycle of manifestation completes itself. There will be an absolute solitary and intense longing.

Allāh! You are the First, the Last, the Seen, the Unseen.

You are the One, the Only.

The Prophet said, "Allāh alone existed before creation," to which our master ʿAlī, companion of the Prophet and the "Door of Knowledge", added that Allāh alone exists even now. Nothing exists other than Him. What is now is what was before; what was then is the same as now. Our occupation and duty as humans is only to maintain constant remembrance of our Lord. So let us be steadfast in giving thanks and praise to Him, resolute in avoiding disbelief, accepting of all that He places upon us. And no matter how busy, complicated, and stressful our lives may become, let us always set aside time for Him, time to seek His Mercy and Forgiveness. When we approach Him, let us come in absolute humility, like a worker who has been avoiding his job. Certainly when the worker decides to return, he would not come arrogantly but only with complete humility.

At this stage, I welcome you all with the warmest of welcomes. In setting aside this day to commemorate the Prophet, we are acknowledging that we are all servants of Allāh. So this is a day for us all to get closer to Him.

There is a relative connection between Allāh's rule (*mulk*) and His kingdom (*malakūt*).[164] An individual, who wants to of-

---

164 *Mulk* and *malakūt* have been translated literally here. However, it is possible the Shaykh's reference to *malakut* is meant to allude to the five presences or planes of existence (*ḥaḍarāt*), in which case *Malakut* refers to the second *ḥaḍra*, the world of similitude (ʿālam al-mithāl) that comprises the seven heavens and the effusion of Divine lights. *Mulk*, then, likely would refer to Allāh's dominion in the ʿālam al-nāsūt, the material world of dense bodies. In any case, the meaning seems to be similar: the material world is

fer something to Allāh, should first be prepared to place the gift in the hands of a human being. One day the Prophet witnessed his wife, ʿĀʾisha, carefully perfume some clothing she was preparing to give to a poor person. When the Prophet asked her about this, she replied that it was first going to Allāh. The Prophet was duly impressed, as he knew that the clothing would indeed reach Allāh first before the poor person. However quick the poor person's hand may be, Allāh's acceptance is faster. If you hold back giving to another human being, to a fellow son of Adam, while still expecting your offering to be accepted by Allāh, from your hand to His, be sure your own gift will be left hanging. Allāh never accepts the request of a miser. When you give even a penny to someone, it will surely reach Allāh, the Creator. Anything a person does for another person is in reality done for Allāh. If someone wants to work for Allāh, he should first work for His servants; if someone wants to give to Allāh, he should first give to His servants.

Since we are all knocking on His door on this special day, I speak on behalf of Allāh Himself in welcoming you all with the greatest of welcomes.

As the servant of Allāh who gives to a beggar is in reality giving to Allāh, he should realize that, even in the act of giving, he is himself the beggar. For by his gift, he is begging at the door of Allāh, seeking entry into His Presence. Once there lived a poor person who had nothing left but a slice of bread. He approached a wealthy and generous king and presented him his slice of bread. Why should the poor man present such a small gift to one who clearly had no need of anything from him? Because the poor man knows of the king's generosity and therefore can expect a much better gift in return for his measly slice of bread. By his gift, the poor man came asking, but in a more courteous manner than merely begging.

---

a symbolic testing ground for higher planes of existence. For more on the subject of the five *ḥaḍarāt*, see Shaykh Ibrāhīm Niasse, *Sirr al-akbar*.

This is similar to the act of sending Allāh's blessings on the Prophet Muḥammad. The Prophet is of course a fellow created being, but he also is the light of creation, to whom Allāh gave everything, including Himself. Indeed, if anybody could claim that his kingdom is greater than that of Allāh, it would have been the Prophet, as Allāh bestowed on him His own person, His attributes, His names, His signs, His singularity and His innumerable manifestations. The only thing Allāh did not give to the Prophet was permission to say, "I am Allāh." Other than that, he deserves all of the exalted titles. Does such a Prophet need our prayers? Does a wealthy king need a slice of bread?

The Prophet needs nothing more from Allāh that we can solicit by our prayers. Allāh has already completed His favor to the Prophet and satisfied him with His own blessing. The invitation to send blessings on the Prophet is nothing but an invitation for us to draw closer to Allāh.

The completion of Allāh's favor on the Prophet Muḥammad is reflected in his righteous manner and generous deeds. As a servant of Allāh, the Prophet never did anything that displeased His Lord. It was simply against his nature, just as it is against the nature of man to fly like a bird. We all bear witness to his personal sacrifices, his unwavering devotion every second of his life for the sake of Allāh. Does this person need our prayers? But if we make any prayers for him, we can be sure they will be accepted and recompensed by Allāh. Can we say the same of our other prayers to Allāh? They are only requests, pleas and entreaties.

As Muslims, our objective here today in gathering for the sake of Allāh is to take away what belongs to us. May Allāh accept us and provide us with our objective! May Allāh give us the best both here and in the hereafter! May He provide us with Himself!

Since the beginning of creation, Allāh Himself has been responsible for guiding His servants to the path of righteousness. Witness how He sent us His Messengers, beginning with Adam and ending with Muḥammad, the Seal of the Prophets. Following them are the scholars (ʿulamāʾ), those who inherit from the Prophets. The Prophet said, "The ʿulamāʾ are those who have inherited from the Prophets, and the Prophets do not leave an inheritance of dirhams or dinars, but only of knowledge." In other words, the scholars are not heirs by wealth or ancestral descent; they are heirs by their hard work and strenuous effort for the sake of Allāh. Otherwise the scholars would only be found among the Arabs and descendants of the Prophet. The Prophet said, "I am the grandfather of every pious Muslim (*mutaqqin*)." Thus, the inheritance of the Prophet is only achievable through an individual's well-intentioned effort and determination. Otherwise, there is no inheritance from the Prophets of Allāh.

Once during a visit to Cairo, I entered the central (Azhar) mosque to pray the Friday Juma'a prayer. As soon as we sat down, the imam approached me with a request to give the sermon (*khutba*). I kept silent for a moment, so he suggested that he could withdraw the proposal until another time. I replied, "If not now, then when?" I ascended the pulpit (*minbar*), gave the *khutba*, and then led the prayer as was expected. Later an Arab king among the congregation asked who led the prayer and was told, to his surprise and admiration, that he was a black man.

In Islam the individual who has more knowledge is the leader. Thus, the imam introduced me afterwards, "This is our honorable guest. We have accepted that he has more knowledge than any of us, and so have given him the responsibility of leading us in prayer. His short sermon reminded us what has been forgotten. He has reawakened in us the sweet melody of the Holy Qurʾān and the admirable characteristics of the previous ʿulamāʾ we long to see. Since the establishment of Azhar University, there has never been an outsider to lead the prayer. It is only done by a scholar who has studied here, but I stress to you again that Islam only considers the most knowledgeable person among us to be the leader."

Once, a descendant (*sharīf*) of the Prophet lived in the same town as a black slave. This slave was so pious that his master was overwhelmed by shame and freed him. After his freedom, this former slave became a great and famous Islamic scholar with many followers. Unlike him, the *sharīf* was a drunkard and caused trouble everywhere he went. One day, in the center of town, when the scholar was walking with a large group of followers, they came face to face. The *sharīf* made his way through the crowd of students until he reached the scholar.

Arrogantly, he said, "You are a black man. Your father was an unbeliever! Look how people honor you while they shun and abuse me, a *sharīf* of the Prophet! Do you consider such a situation justifiable?"

The teacher answered, "Of course you have said the truth. My parents were both unbelievers and I am a black man, as black as black itself. But I have enlightened my heart with the faith of Allāh, a strong faith that has brought light to my skin, body, and soul. People have become attracted to this light, and care little about my black complexion. While your skin is white, your heart has created black patches all over your face so that people can neither see you nor love you as a *sharīf*. While I left my parents' path of error and took the path of your grandfather, you forsake his righteous and glorious path and follow the path of my parents. When the people saw me on your grandfather's path, they embraced, welcomed, and dignified me like the Prophet's son, and when they saw you on my parent's path, they thought of you as the degraded son of unbelievers, one who deserves abuse and disgrace. These are the reasons for the situation you see as unjustifiable. The abuse my followers have accorded you on your way to me is forgivable, but your own drunkenness is a punishable offence according to the Sacred Law. It is only on account of your grandfather that I myself have forgiven you for the unruly manner in which you approached me."

This is the nature of the heritage of the Prophet. A person cannot inherit from him by birth, wealth, status, position or any such things. The Prophet is merely a grateful servant of Allāh. He has no relationship with Allāh except friendship. Therefore, he who chooses the path of the Prophet becomes a friend of Allāh. He who abstains from this path of righteousness has nothing to do with Allāh and his Messenger.

The Prophet Abraham, the father of both Jews and Arabs, is best known as the righteous Pole of Allāh's Oneness (*qutb al-tawhīd*). However righteous a person's father may be, his righteousness cannot be compared to that of the Prophet Abraham. Among the honors given to him was the title, "Pole of Oneness", that Muḥammad was among his descendants, and that it was his followers who were first called "Muslims." So the followers of Muḥammad are also those who follow the path of Father Abraham, which makes all of us his children. Indeed, a person who follows this path has more blessings than the direct child who does not. One of the weaknesses of human nature is to love one's children the most. But we should be on guard to stress righteousness above all else. Sadly, even the children of Prophets, who have been nonetheless honored for the sake of their fathers, have sometimes caused corruption in the teachings of the religion.

Any person who follows this path becomes a child of the Prophet, and any person who does not follow it has nothing to do with him, even if he were a direct child. There are those of the Prophet's family whom Allāh cursed during his lifetime, as the Qur'ān testifies. Abū Laḥab,[165] for example, was from the same parents as 'Abd-Allāh, the father of the Prophet. But even in cursing members of his family, Allāh showed gentle-

165 Abu Lahab is cursed by Allāh in Chapter 111 of the Qur'ān, the first line of which is "Perish be the hands of Abu Lahab..."

ness to His Prophet. Most of the last chapters of the Qur'ān give instructions to the Messenger, commanding him, "Say!" – "*Say: I seek refuge with the Lord and Cherisher of Mankind.*"[166] "*Say: I seek refuge with the Lord of the Dawn.*"[167] And, "*Say: He is Allāh, the One and Only.*"[168] Then comes "*Perish the hands of the Father of the Flame,*"[169] this time without the command "Say". Allāh did not want the Prophet to have to curse his own father's brother, so Allāh did so Himself.

He who lives for Allāh, Allāh will in turn live for him, and so the Prophet Muḥammad will become his "father". This is a fundamental precept in our religion of Islam: the Prophet is the father of every righteous Muslim.

---

166 Qur'ān, 114:1.
167 Qur'ān, 113:1.
168 Qur'ān, 112:1.
169 Qur'ān, 111:1.

"May Allāh Give Us Allāh"

This speech was given at the annual Ziyāra, or gathering of the Shaykh's students in Medina-Baye, Senegal. See the previous description for "The Heritage of the Prophet" for further information on the background to this text.

* * *

This day is a day to give thanks to Allāh. Little do people remember to thank Allāh! And then few of us do so with the proper humility. Iblīs (Satan) has promised to stand in the way of humans to prevent them from thanking Allāh until the majority of them become ungrateful and insatiable. We must constantly be offering gratitude to Allāh. The first declaration of the Qur'ān requires us to say, *al-ḥamdu li-Llāh*, "All Praise is due to Allāh." He is the Creator and Lord of mankind, and despite the fact that most people do not offer gratitude; He is also Oft Forgiving and the Most Merciful. Not the least among us can deny benefiting from His Mercy, yet do we show our gratitude by praising Him? Indeed, only a few offer thanks and praise to Him.

When it rains, it does not rain just on one farm or in one area. Every rain has a specific cause and purpose. Whether it is for a particular person or for a group of people, it still rains on everyone's land. It is the same when you approach Allāh to offer thanks. He accepts not just from you but also from everyone who received the blessings, from everyone who benefited from the rains. Say *al-ḥamdu li-Llāh!*

I wondered how I could find evidence from Allāh that we are going to Paradise as the recipients of Allāh's mercy. Allāh answered from the Holy Qur᾿ān – the book that we all bear witness came from Allāh, the book that guides and directs men toward righteousness, the book that makes men's hearts fear Allāh – that those who believe in the Unseen – the Hereafter, the Resurrection, the Judgment Day, the Bridge, Paradise, and Hellfire – are all recipients of His mercy.

He ordained that we pray the five daily prayers. I observe that we are all steadfast in the ritual prayer. He said we should give charity, and I have witnessed each of you has given out of his property for charity, and has spent of his wealth in order to be here today. Allāh also said that we must believe in what was sent through the Prophets. We believe in the Holy Qur᾿ān and the other Books sent down before the Qur᾿ān. For those who have faith in the whole Truth, without adding or subtracting anything – and we all have faith in this Truth – Allāh said, "Those are the righteous who have succeeded." (78:31). If we can be counted among the righteous, Allāh has promised us Paradise ...

You have come to perform *ziyāra*. But it is not for my sake that you have come, I know you have come only for Allāh. I am not Allāh, but you deserve Allāh of me. When I was not present, you still organized and performed the *ziyāra*. You never stopped coming even though I was not here. The One whom you met here during my absence was Allāh. May Allāh allow you to be present with Him again today even as I am present here with you. May He be with us forever.

In reality, Allāh is everywhere; but His manifestations vary in degrees from one place to another. One student, after arriving in the presence of Allāh (*wuṣūl*), started neglecting his shaykh. He said, "After I have seen Allāh, of what use is my shaykh?" The shaykh answered, "It is better for you to see me once, than to see Allāh a thousand times." You may see Allāh in anything. Allāh can manifest in a tree, in a mosque minaret, in a cow, in a sheep, or even in myself, the one speaking to you now. You can see that they vary greatly in both shape and magnitude. However, All these are the manifestations of the One, the Most High.

When you came to perform *ziyāra* and did not meet me, you met Allāh. He was without doubt here. May Allāh accept your *ziyāra* as He accepted the previous ones, and there is no doubt that he accepted them since they did not contain any arrogance or showing off. But even if you should show pride in the services rendered for your shaykh, this does not necessarily make it bad or poor work. As for myself, I am proud of my work for you and happy for you to see what I am doing. When you came when I was not here, you proved the loyalty and sincerity of your sacrifices just for the sake of Allāh. Actions are judged according to intention. Once a saint made several attempts to go on the Pilgrimage but was unable. When Allāh finally fulfilled his intention, the saint went to Arafat and gave thanks to Allāh, asking Him to accept his pilgrimage, as well as his previous attempted pilgrimages. Making an intention to do something is equal to its accomplishment, even if Allāh does not permit the intention to materialize. The previous *ziyāra* were surely accomplished and accepted. May Allāh accept this present one too, like those performed before.

There are three types of gratitude a Muslim is obligated to offer to Allāh. The first is giving thanks by the tongue, which entails saying *al-ḥamdu li-Llāh* constantly. No matter how much wealth Allāh bestows on a servant, the servant cannot give anything in return except to say *al-ḥamdu li-Llāh*. Consider what Allāh gave to King Solomon, son of David: a vast kingdom; rule over men, *jinn*, animals, birds, reptiles, and insects; control of the oceans and the earth; and, most importantly, Prophethood. No one was ever given more worldly power and prestige than Solomon. And with all of this, he could only say, *al-ḥamdu li-Llāh.*

A certain saint once left his shaykh and traveled to a far land where he attained illumination and became adorned with the radiance of Allāh's light. He was granted a prestigious position with the king of the land and became exceedingly wealthy. Overwhelmed at Allāh's bounty, he wrote to his shaykh asking what more he could say than *al-ḥamdu li-Llāh* to thank Allāh. His shaykh replied that no amount of wealth could surpass the value of *al-ḥamdu li-Llāh*. Indeed, a person who says *al-ḥamdu li-Llāh* should be aware that he has offered the highest form of gratitude expected of him. This is thanking Allāh by the tongue.

The second form of gratitude is thanking Allāh through righteous deeds, by spending wealth in the cause of Allāh. It is incumbent upon every Muslim to spend of his wealth for pious ends. For example, the Muslim with means should be striving to give to the disadvantaged, feed the poor, shelter the orphans, and help build mosques and schools.

Thirdly, a person may also show gratitude through good manners (*adab*). Termed "the gratitude of those who have witnessed", good behavior is acknowledging the Beautiful Countenance of Allāh by constantly witnessing and praising Him. Allāh is a King possessed of incomparable, absolute Beauty, Magnificence, Love and Omnipotence. To Him belong all the most beautiful Names and Attributes. He does not love anyone so much as him who "sees" Him, and none but the gnostics (*ʿārif bi-Llāh*) – the knowledgeable people of Allāh – are seeing Him. They are the knowledgeable saints, for they observe His Beauty and have thus become the grateful ones among us. May Allāh put us among them and allow us to give abundant thanks to Him.

Let us be of firm resolve, for Allāh's Being is without limit, and the ladder leading to Him proceeds to infinity. To travel this path, you must first search out and follow a qualified guide (*murshid*) – not someone who will exploit your trust, but one who wants you to succeed and can guide you until you arrive at the full realization of Allāh's Countenance. Until a Muslim has reached this stage [of annihilation in Allāh], he will not be able to avoid ascribing partners to Allāh (*shirk*). You must also come to know the Prophet, for without knowledge of him, Allāh has little consideration for you. The Prophet Muḥammad is the only doorway to Allāh. He who does not pass through the Prophet, will never reach Allāh. After this, you must strive to know your guide on the path. If a person should neglect this knowledge claiming he has been overtaken by the other stages [of annihilation in Allāh and annihilation in the Prophet Muḥammad], the knowledge of the guide will be concealed from him.[170] I am urging you to strive vigorously for knowledge, first of Allāh, then of these two later stages of His Attributes.

After passing these realities, you shall journey on the path that will return you to the perfection of His Essence (*dhāt*). Here you will be granted full consciousness of Allāh in wakefulness and not just in annihilation or drunkenness. This state will be observed with the eye of certainty. The position of the Prophet and the Shaykh will here be clearly evident, for they are both of the essential realities (*haqā ʾiq*), and their light can-

---

170 In other words, after extinction (*fana'*) in Allāh, the seeker must proceed to extinction in the Prophet Muḥammad and then to the Shaykh. Elsewhere, the Shaykh phrases the same series of annihilations in a slightly different fashion, but the meaning seems to be the same: "The first thing the gnostics are concerned with for the aspirant is to find extinction in Allāh. Then, after that, he ascends until he arrives to extinction in the Shaykh, since the Shaykh is an attribute of Allāh. The request from these two extinctions is that the servant will return to a station where, if he does not meet with the Messenger of Allāh and with the Shaykh, he will not be able to know such a station later on. See Shaykh Ibrāhīm Niasse, *Jawāhir al-Rasā ʾil*, II: 60.

not be disassociated from Allāh's light. In fact, one can hardly differentiate them from the *dhāt* of Allāh.

When I accomplished the first stage of annihilation, I at first concluded that Shaykh Tijānī could not be my teacher. But then Allāh showed me that Shaykh Tijānī is the means to all the accomplishments of the saints, and certainly my master.[171]

The intoxicated ascetic (*majdhūb*) is he who makes seemingly arrogant pronouncements because he has recently become annihilated in Allāh, the Exalted. The one who has freshly arrived at this stage constantly flatters himself into thinking that he is everything and has everything. When Allāh says to him, "I have given you all My Kingdom plus Myself," the individual assumes that Allāh has given to him what He has never given to anyone else. A passerby who happens to overhear such a statement may conclude that it is a nonsensical impossibility, while the ignorant person may believe the speaker to have been endowed with a unique and extraordinary spiritual station (*maqām*). Rather every individual who has passed through this stage of intoxication (*jadhb*) has had the same experience. All of them have stood at the feet of the Real and made the same conclusion, even if Allāh's manifestations inevitably differ from person to person. All have become intoxicated with the same One, Living Allāh.

---

171 Elsewhere, Shaykh Ibrāhīm writes about Shaykh Aḥmad Tijānī: "The Shaykh, my master Aḥmad al-Tijānī (may Allāh be pleased with him) is the inheritor of the Messenger of Allāh, his successor and his hidden assistance, his secret to the entirety of existents, in the seen and unseen worlds, from sempiternity to perpetuity. He is distinguished by the attributes of him from whom he has inherited, as a provision from him, may Allāh bless him and grant him peace. To the Shaykh belongs preference from his presence (*ḥaḍra*), and from the presence of the Bountiful Provider. '*That is the bounty of Allāh, He gives it to whom He wills, and Allāh is the owner of great bounty*' (57:21). He is the confluence (*majma*ʿ) of the saints, and their ocean. No saint drinks or gives to drink except by his ocean, (and this) by the stipulation of his sincerity, as he was told by the master of existence, Allāh's blessing and peace upon him." See *Jawāhir al-rasāʾil*, I: 47-48.

Allāh may manifest in a tree, but the next moment this manifestation will move to another tree, or something else. The manifestations of Allāh are constantly evolving and never at a standstill. Certainly, differences between brothers or sisters in the same family must appear, even though they are from the same parents and have the same blood. Allāh says in the Qur᾿ān, "*You see the mountains you deem to be solid, but they are moving like clouds.*"[172]

At this point, those with knowledge of Allāh will be aware that the body that left its home to come to this conference has passed away, and is not the same that will return to its home later tonight. These people that I mentioned have already arrived in the presence of Allāh and achieved illumination. But those that have not awakened from their state of ignorance will not understand my words. They are only aware of the material aspect of things and have yet to see the Truth, the One, the First, the Last.

We are all the servants of Allāh and all of us are in need of Him. His Person alone is sufficient for us. Anything other than Him will pass out of existence while we die needing more. First, I prayed for Allāh to give us abundant wealth, but later I realized that it does not last. Then I asked for mercy but realized it also does not last. I concluded that if a person would remain free of wants and needs, he should ask only for the *dhāt-Allāh*, Allāh Himself. May Allāh give us Allāh. Anything that He gives us other than Himself, will come to pass, and, as His vicegerents, we are bound to always be in need of Him. May Allāh give us Allāh.

The Prophet Moses prayed, "Allāh, provide me with my sustenance, for that is what I expect from you." Moses was still young at this point because once he became mature he asked Allāh for His Person, saying "*O Lord, show Yourself to me, that*

172 Qur᾿ān, 27:88.

I may gaze upon You."[173] Whatever an individual asks of his Lord may indeed be a necessity at the moment of asking, but Allāh's providing it does not prevent one from needing it again. The only thing that can truly satisfy the servant of Allāh is the possession of Allāh Himself. May Allāh grant us His Person. May Allāh give us Himself. Indeed Allāh has promised this to those of us who request it.

As humans, our needs are certainly exceptional. We need nothing less than Allāh Himself. Other living things are not even aware of the existence of such a need or desire, so their hearts are at rest. The one who is awake – whose heart's eye is open – becomes enraptured by the beauty of Allāh's Countenance and longs for nothing else. Allāh said, "*Mankind was created weak.*"[174] This weakness is the individual's admiration, his love, his longing for Allāh, which creates in him an infinite need for Him. What is left for the people of knowledge? We want only Allāh.

---

173 Qur᾽ān, 17:143.

174 Qur᾽ān, 4:28.

Chapter III

Letters to Disciples

Traveling the Path to Allāh (sulūk)

This letter was written from Kaolack in the year 1929, and addressed first to the Shaykh's disciples Aḥmad Thiam and Mālik Sow, and then "to whomever, among those claiming affiliation to us, who should happen upon it."[175]

* * *

In the name of Allāh, the Beneficent, the Merciful, the Avenger, the Mighty, the Compeller, the Supreme, and peace upon the Messenger, the master (of creation), the servant (of Allāh), who said, "O Fatima! I can avail you nothing before Allāh."[176] ...

Let it be known that two types of people have nothing to do with me, or with this path: an enraptured one (*majdhūb*) who has stopped seeking, and a seeker (*sālik*) who has not become

175 Niasse, *Jawāhir al-rasā'il*, I: 10-12.

176 Ḥadīth related from Abū Hurayrah and 'Ā'isha, found in *Ṣaḥīḥ Muslim*, book 1, Ḥadīths 401-402. The Prophet said these words after the revelation, "And warn thy nearest kindred..." (Qur'ān, 26:214).

enraptured with Allāh.[177] Indeed, these two have remained in their states and stopped their advancement. It is my concern, as you know, that he who wants to be with me in my state (*ḥāl*), should travel my path in both words and actions, by obeying the commands (of Allāh) and eschewing the prohibitions, openly and secretly, and by yearning to arrive at Allāh's pleasure, and that of His Messenger.

As for he who associates with us, yet follows anything in violation of the pure and noble Sharīʿa, miring himself in the forbidden things and leaving the (Divine) commands, I bear witness to Allāh, and I bear witness to all of you, that I have nothing to do with such a person. O Allāh! Surely I am innocent before you from what these (wrongdoers) have fabricated. "*And let those who oppose the Messenger's commandment beware, lest some trial befall them, or a grievous penalty be inflicted on them.*"[178] "*And repent to Allāh, all of you Muslims!*"[179]

As for what I told you about my disciples being a receptacle filled up with the secrets of the three audiences (*ḥaḍarāt*),[180] yes indeed. But where is my (true) disciple compared to you? Among you, he is more rare than the red sulfur (*al-kabrīt al-aḥmar*).

---

177 Both *majdhūb* and *sālik* have specific connotations in a Sufi context. The *majdhūb* is one who has become enchanted, bewildered, enraptured or who has otherwise lost his senses and memory of self in the Majesty and Beauty of Allāh. The *sālik* is literally one who travels the path. In setting the two words in opposition, the Shaykh is also speaking to the danger of diligent striving on the path and immersion in its details without witnessing the wonders of the Divine Presence.

178 Qurʾān, 24:63.

179 Qurʾān, 24:31.

180 The Shaykh is here either referring to the realities (*haqāʾiq*) of spiritual initiation (*tarbiya*), or the three stations (*manāzil*) of the religion: submission (Islam), faith (Iman) and spiritual excellence (Ihsan) referred to in the Ḥadīth. More on this subject can be found in Shaykh Ibrāhīm Niasse's *Sirr al-Akbar*, or the treatise, *Maqāmāt al-dīn al-thalāth*.

If the matter is as you have described it,[181] speedily will I revoke the authorization (*idhn*) from every teacher (*muqaddam*) who does not act when forbidden things are committed in his presence. If powerless to act, let him emigrate to Allāh, His Messenger and to us. I swear to Allāh, the end of those who do not respect the Sharīʿa is the accidental return to the blasphemy of incarnation (*ta'annus*). Those who have spent a long period of acquaintance with us have surely learned respect for the Sharīʿa, for who is present with us for a good amount of time forgets the nourishment of vain desires. There are young men here who have indeed forgotten the nourishment of vain desires. Some of them have even forgotten their wives and would not come to them except by permission and command (from us). Such are my students, as for others, no. You must return to Allāh with repentance, obedience, modesty, eschewal, abstinence (*zuhd*), piety and learning. The Most High has said to the friend of friends (the Prophet), "And say, O Lord, increase me in knowledge."[182]

The disciple must not stop in his way until he meets me, and if I cannot change his state, he may travel to a shaykh whose station is above mine. But you should know, may Allāh have mercy on you, that many of those who claim such ascendancy do nothing but prevent people from the path of Allāh through their lack of steadfastness (*istiqāma*). Whoever would attach himself to Allāh while becoming an obstacle on His path, Allāh has marked him with war, and he is among the people of denial and misery. And he (the wrongdoer) is himself the reason for that. It is incumbent upon you to be present with us many times so that you may take from us the proper behavior of seeking (ādāb al-sulūk), just as you took from us the realities of rapture (*jadhb*). And whoever does this will have achieved a great success.

---

181 This letter was written during the early years of the Shaykh's public teaching, in 1349 A.H. (1930), clearly in response to reports that some of those claiming to be his followers were not following the letter of the Law.

182 Qurʾān, 20:114.

It is incumbent upon you to change whatever abominations happen among the brothers, by the hand, the tongue and the heart, as is in the Ḥadīth. Make the ritual prayer, pay the alms, fast the month of Ramadan, and make the pilgrimage to the Sacred House, whoever is able. Give in charity of your wealth for the sake (*wajh*) of Allāh the Most High. In a Ḥadīth related by Muslim from the Messenger of Allāh,

> *Purity is half of faith, and the praise of Allāh fills up the scale. "Glory be to Allāh" and "Praise be to Allāh" fills what is between the heavens and the earth. Prayer is light. Patience is illumination. The Qur'ān is a proof for you or against you. Every person comes as the purchaser of his soul, either enslaving it or setting it free.*[183]

Allāh has said, and He is the most truthful of speakers, "*Surely Allāh commands justice and excellence, and helping kin, and forbids evil, abomination and oppression.*"[184]

So woe to those who do not accept the rule of Allāh and His messenger with total acceptance. But whoever receives our letter and repents and corrects what he can, to him belongs the happiness of the two abodes. Allāh forgives what has passed. But as for him who does not change his ways, Allāh and you are my witness, I have nothing to do with him, and I do not declare my renunciation of anyone except after Allāh and His Messenger have declared renunciation of him. [...]

You must stay away from the idle words of the people (speaking openly) of Divine realities. Seek the straight path. These vain desires are idols, which you worship after claiming to have faith. The Most High has said, "*Whoever disbelieves in idols and believes in Allāh, has grasped a most trustworthy handhold that never breaks, and Allāh is the All Hearing, the All Knowing.*"[185]

---

183 Ḥadīth on the authority of Abu Malik al-Harith, related in *Ṣaḥīḥ Muslim*; also in Imam Nawawī's collection of forty Ḥadīth.

184 Qur'ān, 16:19.

185 Qur'ān, 2:256.

Fear of Allāh (taqwā)

This letter, written at Shaykh Ibrāhīm's request by his closest disciple, ʿAlī b. al-Ḥasan Cissé in 1929, was addressed to some of the Shaykh's early disciples in Senegal.[186]

* * *

In the Name of Allāh, the Compassionate, the Merciful. May Allāh's blessing be on our master Muāammad, and peace as well upon his family and companions.

Praise be to Allāh, who made the following of His saints (*awliy*ā) a source of happiness and righteousness; (who made) the love and exaltation of them, and the obedience to their commands, a source of profit and success. And peace upon the master of the two worlds, who said, "Islam was built on five pillars: witnessing (there is no god but Allāh and that Muḥammad is His Messenger), the five daily prayers, fasting, alms-giving and the pilgrimage for those who are able."[187] And

186 Niasse, *Jawāhir al-rasāʾil*, I: 7-9.

187 Ḥadīth on the authority of Ibn ʿUmar, related in Bukhārī and Muslim; also one of Imam Nawawī's Forty Ḥadīth.

may Allāh be pleased with the Prophet's absolute inheritor (*khalīfatihi ʿalā l-iṭlāq*: Shaykh Aḥmad Tijānī), who said, "If you hear something from me, weigh it on the scale of the Sacred Law (Sharīʿa). If it balances, take it; if it differs, leave it." [...]

Peace be to you all and the mercy and blessing of Allāh, a greeting carrying the support of our master, Shaykh Aḥmad Tijānī. After this, we ask Allāh that He grant righteousness to all our states of being, and to your states, and to our livelihood and to yours. May He provide us with the sweetness of faith, and truthfulness in servant-hood, so that we may stand up for the rights belonging to Allāh. And may He write our names and yours in the register of his beloved and chosen ones. And may He allow us to turn to Him, for to Him is the turning of the righteous.

I am advising you and myself with what Allāh has advised you and the communities before you: and that is the fear (*taqwā*) of Allāh secretly and openly. *Taqwā* means to obey the command of Allāh and avoid His prohibition. I emphasize among His commandments the observance of the five daily prayers, in congregation at the proper time, while guarding your cleanliness (*ṭahāra*) by washing with water. The ultimate arrogance is for one to affiliate himself with Allāh and our Shaykh Tijānī while being heedless of his ritual prayer or its proper conditions of purity. For example, some make the ablution with sand, falsely claiming to be excused from ablution with water.[188] Such a valid excuse does not remain (for more than one prayer), nor can it be generalized to a whole group.

188 The Shaykh is here referring to a subtlety in the jurisprudence of ablution. Dispensation for ablution with water is granted for those who cannot find any (as in the desert), but it cannot be used where water is available. The Shaykh is likely referring to a practice among some Mauritanians to persist in making ablution with sand (*tayyamun*) despite the availability of water.

"*Surely we are from Allāh and to Him we are returning!*"[189] "*So repent to your Creator, and kill your nafs (selves), that is better for you with your Creator.*"[190] There is no escape from renewing your repentance (*tawba*) to Allāh, at all times and in every position. You must be observant of Allāh at all times and with every breath, acting on the saying of the Prophet: "Hold yourselves to account before you are brought to account."

Strive for truthfulness in the affairs of your Lord and Master in such a manner that not one of you is found where He has forbidden you to be, nor absent from where He has commanded you to be. Keep yourself and your close relations away from anything to do with what is unlawful (*harām*). Indeed, the unlawful things neighbor the Fire. Beware of heedlessness, for it is the source of all mistakes, lust and ugly behavior (*sū' adab*). The Exalted and Ultimate Truth says, 'For him to whom I have unveiled My Names, I obligate him with exemplary conduct (ādāb), and for him to whom I have unveiled the perfection of My Essence (*dhāt*), I obligate him with (his self's) destruction (*'aṭab*).' So be careful to observe the proper conduct of seeking (*sulūk*) Allāh. As has been said in verse:

An enraptured one (majdhūb) becomes rebellious if he does not sober up

If he has not corrected himself with obedience, he has abandoned guidance

And who would obtain what is desired, must strive to be thankful

If not, his soul's severance [from the Divine presence] is (only) the beginning of his ruin.

You must work for (the countenance) of Allāh by rejecting everything apart from Him. Encourage each other in

189 Qur'ān, 2:156.
190 Qur'ān, 2:54.

patience, love each other, guide each other, visit each other, spend freely on each other, and sit with each other; (all this) in (the presence of) Allāh, for (the sake of) Allāh, and by (the help of) Allāh. Cooperate with one another in righteousness (*birr*) and piety (*taqwā*), and remember Allāh often so that you may prosper. Save yourselves and your families from the Fire. The Prophet said, "This (saving) is to say, 'O my family, (make) your prayers, your prayers! O my family, (remember) your fasting, your fasting! O my family, (guard) your purity! O my family, (provide for) the indigent among you!" As the Most High has said, "Enjoin on your family the ritual prayer, and to seek patience (in its performance). We do not ask from you provision, rather it is We who provide for you, and the good end belongs to those who are pious (*al-'āqaba li l-taqwā*)."[191]

Know that praise and gratitude to Allāh is incumbent on you, for He made you among the forerunners of this Flood (*fayḍa*). But beware of sitting down and drifting toward complacency. Behind you are a people that will come after you. If you sit, you will fall short in fulfilling the rights of your Lord, and they will overtake you. This would be a great loss, and the refuge is with Allāh. The demand should be for increased spiritual elevation in every moment. So construct your hall of remembrance (*zāwiya*) with the performance of the five prayers and with the congregational remembrance (*waẓīfa*). Fill your time with prayer on the Messenger of Allāh, peace and blessings upon him, with "the prayer of opening what was closed" (*ṣalāt al-fātiḥ limā ughliq*). Whoever does this has attained a great success.

191 Qur'ān, 20:132.

Scholarly Disagreement (ikhtilāf)

The following text is an excerpt from a lesson Shaykh Ibrāhīm gave during the month of Rabīʿ al-Awwal in the Hijri year 1357 (May, 1938), most likely in Medina-Baye.[192] *While the topic appears at first to be an explanation of the Qurʾān chapter al-ʿAṣr, it turns to discuss the method for calling people to Islam, emphasizing that the call must be made by people who share a particular group's identity. The Shaykh then mentions how to address differences.*

* * *

Differences (*khilāf*) are not prohibited. Indeed, humanity was created for the purpose of difference. "*They do not cease to differ, except those to whom your Lord has shown mercy. For this end they were created.*"[193]

192 Niasse, *Jawāhir al-rasāʾil*, II: 110-111.

193 Qurʾān, 11:118-119.

The disagreement (*ikhtilāf*) of the scholars is a mercy.[194] What is prohibited and blameworthy is division (*tafarruqa*), not disagreement. An individual can have one understanding, and another can have a different understanding, so they will naturally disagree. But this is not blameworthy (*madhmūm*). Rather, the blameworthy is what induces negativity in people's hearts. If two understandings should differ, the person (whose opinion differs) should not be censured, since it is not simply a question of one person being right and the other wrong. Indeed, consensus between scholars is perhaps best when it does not preclude (harmless) disagreement, the kind that bears no negative influence (on the hearts of Muslims).

Disagreement befell the companions (of the Prophet). Likewise, if you examine closely the bases of disagreement (among the scholars) you find (only) slight differences therein. But when Satan and the ego (*nafs*) get involved, slight disagreements become severe, and divisions are created between men. Satan and the ego are the enemies of religion, and (because of them), you find communities divide over slight disagreements. In this way, these enemies of religion create discord between people.

If you look closely at the causes for disagreement between the different groups of Islam – the *Khawārij*, the *Shīʿa*, and the *Ahl al-Sunna wa l-Jamāʿa* – you will find the differences very slight indeed. The same is sometimes true for the Sufi orders. But sadly, the lack of any real division does not prevent them from disliking each other, envying each other, and contending with each other. [...]

The (Tijāniyya) Path (*ṭarīqa*) has conditions of which you are all aware. Severance is only realized on the one who actively repudiates the *ṭarīqa*, visits a (non-Tijānī) saint for the sake of spiritual affiliation, or adds a litany (*wird,* of another Sufi

194 Shaykh Ibrāhīm is of course referring to the well-known saying attributed to the Prophet Muḥammad: "Difference of opinion in my community is a mercy."

order) to the Tijānī litany. The evidence for this is that Shaykh al-Tijānī, throughout his whole life and despite the plentitude of his disciples, only ever cut off three people. He said, "The Messenger of Allāh, peace and blessings upon him, ordered me to take away the permission from two men who visited the master (*mawlānā*) ʿAbd al-Salām b. Mashīsh."[195] [...]

The aspirant who takes this *ṭarīqa* is not harmed, nor is his spiritual provision (*madad*) and affiliation to the Shaykh severed, whether he knows his chain of initiators or not. Surely you see that even a person in the Qadiriyya Sufi order derives benefit from Shaykh al-Tijānī, for the provision (*madad*) of all the saints is from him. Evidence for this is the Shaykh's words, "No saint drinks or gives to drink except from our ocean" – even if a person thinks he is deriving benefit from ʿAbd al-Qādir al-Jilānī. In other words, not knowing about Shaykh al-Tijānī does not harm a person. Shaykh al-Tijānī was once asked about a shaykh who is sometimes joined with Allāh's Messenger, and other times joined with him (al-Tijānī). He said, "This is one and the same."

Once Mawlūd Fāl[196] asked his shaykh Muḥammad al-Ḥāfiẓ[197] whether he should make him his shaykh, or make Shaykh al-Tijāni his shaykh. Muḥammad al-Ḥāfiẓ said to him, "If you say that Shaykh al-Tijānī is your shaykh, then he is your shaykh. And if you say that I am your shaykh, you are not misled. Should an aspirant come to me and say, 'I do not know (any shaykh) except you, and I do not want anything except

---

195 ʿAbd al-Salām b. Mashīsh (d. 1227) was from the environs of Tangier, Morocco. His tomb is located on Jabal al-ʿĀlam, where many disciples of the Shādhiliyya still make pious visitation. Ibn Mashīsh was the shaykh of Abu l-Ḥasan al-Shādhilī.

196 Mawlūd Fāl (d. 1851) was a Mauritanian scholar who was among the first to proselytize the Tijāniyya throughout West Africa.

197 Muḥammad al-Ḥāfiẓ al-Shinqīṭī (d. 1830) was one of fourteen disciples of Shaykh al-Tijānī granted full authorization to spread the Tijāniyya during the lifetime of the founder. Al-Ḥāfiẓ was a prominent Islamic scholar from the Idaw ʿAlī tribe of Mauritania, and his affiliation to the Tijāniyya was largely responsible for his tribe's later adoption of the new Sufi order.

from you;' and another should come and say to me, 'I do not know you except as my intermediary': these two are the same so long as they are connected by an authentic transmission (*sanad*). So the two aspirants are one so long as they have taken from a guiding shaykh." [...]

I know that the truthful aspirant has his place close (to me) in (Medina-Baye) Kaolack (Senegal). If the (Tijānī) disciples have built gardens (of spiritual fruits), it (Medina-Baye) is the greatest garden. If they have come with gifts, it (Medina-Baye) is the most abundant gift. When I meet with him (the aspirant) in (this) place, he tells me, "I want nothing except the secret of the Prophet."[198] And that is perfect conduct.

A palm tree is planted (in my garden), and dates appear. A person eats from them and says, "I ate from the fruit of *the* tree." If this should happen but the person does not attribute them to my hospitality, he has still eaten from me. This is the same as a person saying that he has eaten from the fruit of *my* date palm. If this is the same, then surely the one who has taken (spiritual sustenance) from me directly is the same as the one who has taken from one who took from me.

This (difference) should not affect the hearts, nor lead to separation, severance, or mutual contention. Our desire is not this worldly abode. Our desire is Allāh, majestic and exalted. [...] Difference is not prohibited; rather the (negative) influence of difference is prohibited. All of us differ from each other, and our goal in that is the explanation of the Real.

All of the Muslims are a brotherhood. Perhaps people will have different understandings, but that is not a reason for differentiation (*tafarruqa*).

198 *Sirr al-Nabī*. According to Shaykh al-Tijānī Cissé (interview with author, Medina-Baye, Senegal, December 25, 2014), this means: "The aspirant's annihilation in the Prophet is the same as his annihilation in his shaykh. But the perfection of the aspirant's conduct (*adab*) is that he should find all he requires from the presence of the Prophet in the presence of his shaykh."

Spiritual Illumination (fatḥ)

This letter, written in Rabīʿ al-Thānī of the Hijri year 1354 (July, 1935), was originally addressed to Shaykh Ibrāhīm's Mauritanian disciple "Shaykhān" Manna Abba.[199]

* * *

As for what you mentioned concerning the spiritual arrival of the aspirants (*wuṣūl al-murīdīn*), may Allāh be praised for the Muslim community's increase in faith. As for the method of training the others about whom you asked, know, may Allāh guide us and you, that spiritual training in this Sufi path (*ṭarīqa*) is only by the compelling aspiration (*himma*) of the Seal of Saints, Shaykh (Aḥmad) al-Tijānī, may Allāh be pleased with him. It was he who said, "Who would know me, must know me by me alone." The licensed instructor should do no more than to transmit the remembrance, and to communicate only what he has been commanded to communicate regarding the conditions and conduct (of the path).

---

199 Niasse, *Jawāhir al-rasāʾil*, I:24-25.

As for the aspirant (*murīd*), there is nothing for him to do except to guard the known religious obligations and bind himself to the remembrance (*wird*). He must believe that the obligatory remembrance (*al-wird al-lāzim*) is the greatest of the secrets in the Tijāniyya, and the hastening (of arrival) is found therein. After that, let him implement what he is able of the additional remembrances according to what he has been granted permission. He should desire nothing by his devotions except the countenance of Allāh, the Bountiful. He desires neither this world nor the next, and no rank (*maqām*) among the ranks, witnessing the favor as is. He has the best of thoughts (of Allāh), and he entrusts his affairs completely to Allāh. If he persists in this, without any other goal, he will be praising Allāh continuously.

The ugliness in the aspirant – the one calumnious in worship, the great destitute, the depravity among depravities of the ego (*nafs*) – is that Allāh's creation should worship Him and remember Him and expect, by reason of this worship, the illumination (*fatḥ*); whether today or tomorrow, or in a week or month, or in a year. Indeed! No one deserves anything from Allāh, but He deserves worship for His sake alone (*bidhātihi*).

So whoever feels illumination is slow to come, he must repent to Allāh. He should know that if he persisted in his work for the extent of the world's entire lifespan, and he attained illumination for a single moment, he would realize in this moment all what Allāh would teach him of the (Divine) Presence, equal to that and more. And if He should not grant him illumination at all, it is sufficient for him to work for Allāh until he dies. There is nothing for the aspirant to do except to praise Allāh in every state.

Among the brethren, none will remain (in this initial stage) except those who have become senile, according to the will of Allāh. Whose grave is here, he must be buried in it. Whose grave is elsewhere will not be buried here.

"Be for Allāh!"

This letter is the first of those included in Shaykh Ibrāhīm's collection, "The Pearls of Letters."[200] *It was written in Kossi, a farm outside of Kaolack, Senegal, in the Hijri year 1348 (1929), and addressed to Muḥammad Muṣṭafā b. Jorn Sām (Thiam), one the Shaykh's early disciples.*

* * *

I am entrusting you to Allāh, whose safekeeping is eternal. I am advising you to attach your heart to Allāh in each moment of movement and rest. And be for Allāh! Whoever is for Allāh, Allāh is for him, and He will bring out the entirety of the creation for your affairs in service to the Truth, as you yourself are from the whole of creation.

"*Say, Allāh! Then leave them plunged in (their) trifling.*"[201] You should know, Allāh has ordained that your occupying

200 Niasse, *Jawāhir al-rasāʾil*, I: 5-6.

201 Qurʾān, 6:91.

yourself with anything other than Him is just wallowing (in abasement) and trifling play.

Know that you have two shaykhs. Your external shaykh is the Qur ʾān and the Sunna. Your internal shaykh is our Shaykh Aḥmad al-Tijānī, may Allāh be pleased with him, and he is with you always. But the means are only the means, and the goal is (Allāh) as I have said.

Hide your secret. Bury what Allāh has entrusted with you from the secret of His lordship, until Allāh makes you appear. He who would be a shaykh before the existence of permission from Allāh has lost his religion and his (portion in the) world, and he will be degraded among the sons of his species.

And if Allāh makes you appear, no one can prevent His gift. But the love of appearance before its (proper) time severs the very appearance of Divine favor, since the ego has a portion therein. So if Allāh has obscured you, then obscurity is better for you. And if Allāh has made you appear, then that is better for you. Do not want anything except what Allāh wants. For whoever wants to appear (before the people), he is the worshipper of appearance, and whoever wants to be obscured (from the people), he is a worshipper of obscurity. But whoever wants nothing except what Allāh wants is a true worshipper of Allāh. The one who knows Allāh (ʿārif) is he who has left his own desires for the desire of the Real.

Chapter IV

Arabic Poetry

Tears into Pearls

The following selection is from Taysīr al-wuṣūl ilā ḥaḍrat al-rasūl ("Facilitating the Arrival to the Prophetic Presence").[202] *Taken from the first section, "ḥarf alif", these are the opening lines of the Shaykh's most well known collection of poetry, al-Diwāwīn al-sitt.*

* * *

Enslaved in love, the heart turns away from everything else

Bound in longing for the Prophet, bewildered

I spent an entire night sleepless, singing poetry

In remembrance of him who was pure goodness from beginning to end

So I write (these verses) at night, while my neighbors sleep

And from my eyes tears rain down.

---

202 Niasse, *al-Dawāwīn al-sitt* (Beirut: Dār al-fikr, 2012), 7-8.

Describing him is like arranging pearls to form words

A pearl perfectly formed: he is the full moon

Muḥammad is the key to all illuminations, my master

He is the seal of all Messengers, their end and their predecessor

By him did all Prophets obtain their needs

By him are the cosmological presences adorned, so venerate and exalt him!

* * *

If you should ask concerning my beloved and my master–

Surely it is Ṭā-Hā, the beloved of Allāh, and none other

Every moment I have disposed in remembrance of him

Invoking blessings and praise; so from him I became illustrious

Who competes with me in ardent love for our Prophet

Has desired a thing impossible and forbidden

Like the one who wanted to catch the moon stretching out his fingers

Or to bring back yesterday today.

Ruby of the Creation

This is a brief selection from "ḥarf tā'" of the poem, Iksīr al-sa'āda fī madḥ sayyid al-sādāt ("The Elixir of Happiness in Praise of the Master of Masters").[203] *It is followed by several lines from the poem, Salawat al-shujūn fī madḥ al-nabī al-ma'mūn ("The Relief of Anxieties in the Praise of the Guarded Prophet").*[204]

* * *

I reflected on him who is the sustenance (qūt) for all of creation

They are stones, but the chosen one (muṣṭafa), the master, is a ruby

For he is the manifestation of Allāh's essential being (dhāt), indeed he is His eye ('ayn)

So the exalted sovereignty (mulk) is through him, as well as the realm of command (malakūt).

* * *

203 Niasse, *al-Dawāwīn al-sitt*, 39.

204 Niasse, *al-Dawāwīn al-sitt*, 86-87.

Surely the Messenger is Allāh's praise (*madḥ*) and His spirit (*rūḥ*)
So say of him what you like, do not fear exceeding the limits

As you have said that he is Allāh's servant, and the master of creation
Then attribute to him what you will, and do not fear infidelity (*kufr*)

He is everything, and truly everything is from him
In pre-eternity, Allāh chose him and gave to him without constraint

He came first, testifying to Allāh's Oneness, the first to remember
The first remembered, and the Lord granted him the night journey

All affairs belong to him and return to him
Beloved of Allāh the Creator, and the command was entrusted to him

To him belong my head, my face, my beard
My outside, my inside, the (blood) that flows (between); my complete devotion

I come to you a slave, if you should so exalt me in offering myself
Surely I see this (as a gift) from you, my pride

Remembering the Prophet

This is one of the early sections, "ḥarf rā'", of *Taysīr al-wuṣūl.*[205]

* * *

Yearning for Mustafa the Chosen
Infused my internal being
All I am, and every molecule I am
He is my secret and my manifestation

When the full moon is filled with light
I am filled with his remembrance
I remember him in everything seen
In every contemplation

205 Niasse, *al-Dawāwīn al-sitt*, 14-15.

I remember him in every melody

In every sweetness

He is my life, the taste in my mouth

And my intoxication

In every trial and victory

I remember him

I remember him when I am present

And in the self's annihilation

In the company of beloveds

I remember him

Nor did I forget him

At the foreigners' vexation

I have never seen beauty

Other than his face

There is no beauty save his face

The one shrouded in meditation

My aspiration, existence, is for Mustafa

I the eye of his essence

Otherwise, in him let my death
Be my race's passionate dedication

If not for Paradise's delight
By his light
No longing would have the enlightened
For the eternal accommodation

If it had been Allāh's Emissary
To ignite (Hellfire)
For me every kindled flame
Would be an eternal incineration

O to be as the two grandsons
Hugging his prostrated back
Or like the truthful (Abu Bakr)
Or Ja'far in close association

And would that I were now
The sand under his sandals
A toothbrush for the trustworthy
Bearer of glad proclamation

Would that I were his draught
Water from the cup
And the cupbearer for him
The herald, bearer of illumination

Longing for reunion
My hope is in him
His communion overflows the servant
Sincere in divine consecration

Blessings on Yā Sīn, Ṭā Hā
Muḥammad
And his family and companions
In eternal continuation.

Visiting the Beloved

This is "ḥarf mīm" from the poem *Manāsik ahl al-wadād fī madḥ khayr al-ʿibād* ("The Hermitage of Lovers in the Praise of the Best of Worshippers").[206] The poem was written on one of the Shaykh's later visits to the Prophet's tomb in Medina, Arabia.

* * *

Love of the Hashemite (Prophet) has filled the heart, so I did not sleep

While in Paris, and around me the heedless slept; but mine is not to blame

All the beauties of existence are eclipsed suddenly

When the loved one appears

206 Niasse, *al-Dawāwīn al-sitt*, 199-202.

Now the lights, the colors, the dancing, the singing

Remind the seers of the confluence of blessing

The palaces of kings, the hunting grounds, the bridges, the flags

Are but a reminder of him in whom prophecy has been sealed

The time (in Paris) did not make me forget the dwelling of goodness (Medina)

In which every bondsman of the Guardian Lord is like the (common) servant

And the time did not make me forget the moment of my farewell

To Aḥmad, while I overflowed in tears

And the time did not make me forget the prayer niche of Aḥmad

Nor his magnificent pulpit, grand beacon of light

And the time did not make me forget the moment when I sat

With the noble Aghwāt,[207] *and my thoughts became dazzled*

And I entered the Blessed Paradise, though I had not died

This by the favor of my beloved, the loftiest of blessings

---

207 Aghwāt was a bench on the southern end of the Prophet's mosque where the Ahl al-Suffah were said to congregate.

I must say (to him), with all shyness and humility

Out of complaint, my heart in pain

O Messenger of Allāh! See this inattentive servant burdened with sin

And besides you there is nothing to seek

There has not come a servant like I so full of crimes[208]

To visit your tomb, no matter from what time or community

Those of my generation have matured, but my faults have increased

What calamity! For disobedience and old age to have been combined

And what catastrophic disobedience, remaining protected and covered in favors

While committing sins, however small

If the time were to bear what this servant is carrying

All the vast expanses would have become dark with sin and oppression

---

208 This claim of sinfulness is part of the genre of Prophetic praise poetry and is meant to accent the author's reliance on Divine grace rather than his own works. It is certainly not a confession of violations of the Islamic sacred law.

O my Lord! Forgive me and guide my heart to love

Him whom You love, the chosen one of all the nations

Him by whom You guide all species of Your creation

Him by whom You raise the flag of Islam and smash the idols

Increase this servant in noble knowledge

Stand him in the presence of Mustafa, so he may greet the chosen one

Greetings to the Messenger, Muḥammad

Greetings to Ta Ha, greetings to the confluence of favors

Greetings to he who wiped away deviation, he who spread the good news

Greetings to the guide, him by whom the water gushes out

Greetings to the Prophet of Light, the most trustworthy

Throughout my life, I have taken the praise of Mustafa as my allotment

Greetings to the (Divinely) guarded one, Aḥmad my helper

Greetings to the praised one; while the flames of passion burn bright

Greetings from this lover, filled with shortcomings

Whose deeds do not verify his claim to love the purest one among all peoples

Greetings from the lover, whose destination has become far
So he started greeting the best of mankind with his pen

Greetings to him from this adoring servant
While flying in the air over Europe
Greetings to him from Paris,
While the players of Marseilles win their victory

On a plane, with Christians all around me
But I am in Medina the radiant, for how many needs I have there!

Peace from Allāh, exalted is His Majesty
On Mustafa, who is watching this servant and smiling

The Creator is spreading the good news of my praise poem
And the chosen of creation is pleased with this servant, and has not blamed him

So despite my offenses, I became one of the favored
The beloved of Allāh's Messenger among the retinue of those who serve him

Like this I arrived at the shortcut to all spiritual stations, flying
To a Presence by which all veils are shattered

By this I lost myself
In the Divine Beauty and Majesty, which renders all else non-existent

By this I became alive for the duration of time itself, eternal remaining
I was liberated from impurities, from evil and sickness

By Him, to Him, in Him, from Him is my disposition of authority
My will is the Will of the Real, and the servant is as the Pen

Sometimes I am at the House of Allāh, and sometimes
At the place of Mustafa, the Praiseworthy, and the heart has caught fire

And sometimes I am with the pure companions of Paradise, and sometimes
I am engrossed with the people; but all has become non-existent

In that place, those who want to benefit me are the same
As those who want to do me harm. I am not afraid nor do I find blame

Praise and Peace on Aḥmad the Chosen, from the Presence of his Lord

(A prayer) by which the wrath is averted

Praise and Peace (to him) throughout the ages, thankful I am
For the favors of the Lord: gratitude is due to Him throughout the ages

On him the prayer of Allāh, then peace
These salutations and poetry are favors to be thankful

On him the prayer of Allāh, then peace
Accept me, O Chosen One

On him the prayer of Allāh, then peace
Protect me from blindness, sterility, dumbness and weakness

On him the prayer of Allāh, then peace
Protect me from the evil of poverty, ignorance and illusion

On him the prayer of Allāh, then peace
Protect me from the evil of debt, misfortune and depression

On him the prayer of Allāh, then peace

Protect me from the evil of avarice, greed and confusion

On him the prayer of Allāh, then peace

Protect me from the evil of injustice, guile and false accusations

On him the prayer of Allāh, then peace

And guard my children, save them from affliction

On him the prayer of Allāh, then peace

Make my city a light for the world

On him the prayer of Allāh, then peace

Grant my companions the blessings for which they aspire

On him the prayer of Allāh, then peace

So the Fire does not touch those who know and understand me

On him the prayer of Allāh, then peace

What I want for my religion is well known

On him the prayer of Allāh, then peace

Here in the Far West I bring life to you, O confluence of blessing

On him the prayer of Allāh, then peace

By this prayer I obtain intimacy in the rotting grave

Back to my country, I return repenting to the Creator

Seeking forgiveness of the Lord for what He knows (of my condition)

Upon him and his noble family and companions, blessings and peace

Like the rain, in light drops, and in blinding torrents

Spiritual Training

The following verses are selected from poems included in chapter six of Kāshif al-ilbās concerning spiritual training (tarbiya).[209] *Unlike many other poems in this book, Shaykh Ibrāhīm authored these verses himself. Instructors and disciples still recite such poems to remind themselves of the comportment required on the spiritual path.*

* * *

Some advice for the one coming to me in attentive audition,

The one urgently seeking the way of guidance:

Let him take the path of the Shaykh (al-Tijānī), with permission of its folk

Not all of them are the same, so keep company with one emulated

209 Niasse, *Kāshif al-ilbās ʿan fayḍat al-khatm Abī l-ʿAbbās* (Cairo: al-sharika al-dawliyya, 2001), 116-118. I have adapted the translations here slightly from those included in the original translation of the *Kāshif*, found in *The Removal Confusion Concerning the Saintly Seal Aḥmad al-Tijānī* (Kentucky: Fons Vitae, 2010), 92-95.

This litany is naught but asking forgiveness, declaring Allāh's Oneness,

And blessings on the Chosen One; then avoiding combining (litanies)

The heart's attentiveness is a condition, and withstraining the idle glance

Cast about in the creation; so listen to this advice and find protection

Rely only on the grace (faḍl) of our Lord

You are no benefit to yourself, so full of limitations

Like this, witness the favors of Allāh

But toil not to become wrapped in fanciful curiosities; rather be compliant

Think well of Allāh, whatever may happen

Entrust everything to Him; be crushed in trembling fear

Blessings and peace from the Real, for all time

On the first existent, the last gatherer

* * *

Leave behind your dwellings and the beautiful women

Leave the laden tables and soft couches

And keep company with any master successful in combining

The Sacred Law (sharīʿa) and the Divine Reality (ḥaqīqa)

A brother, pious and ascetic, uninterested

In anything beyond what is right and proper

Beware of vain desires, and beware

The brother wrapped up in the passing of time

(To the pious teacher) grant sovereign leadership, since you know

There is none above him in this affair

Certainly he has obliterated external appearance

And has been made to arrive in the Presence of Holiness

Brought close, sanctified, and summoned

By Divine permission, with the speech of everything near (to Allāh)

When you see such a man, congratulations to you on the occasion of arrival

For seeing him is a most glorious treasure to the eyes

So the blessing of Allāh, together with peace

Upon the chosen one, from the first to the last

* * *

I advise you all, fellow companions

To be patient and forgive your brethren

Do not concern yourself with hearsay

Occupy the heart with the Prayer of Opening (ṣalāt al-fātiḥ)

You will then know, whatever is willed

By Allāh is; and affairs are not according to your whims.

* * *

Beware of your egos, if you would be rightly guided

The one astray cannot harm the guide

When (the ignorant) tell you, "You are in error,"

Content yourself with knowledge of the Majestic Guardian Lord.

If the brother of communion should sever the communion

We fret not, for our communion is with the Guardian Lord

And if you should happen upon their (calumnious) talk, be generous

The brother of perfection is not diminished by words

* * *

O enraptured one: do not travel (this path)
For your own sake; but rather for the sake of the Real, Most High
Do not travel from non-existence, for the sake of non-existence!
That is the work of a foolish, blind man

Indeed this lower world
All of it, including the world on high
Contains nothing that can bring benefit or cause harm:
To meet with the One who causes, leave aside the cause

Betake yourself to Allāh, do not trouble yourself
With other than Him: such is the devotion (taqwā) of the saint
The matter is not about the discovery of created things
Or about spying into unseen affairs

Allāh is nearer, more exalted and more majestic
Spend your time with Allāh, the Glorious
And invoke blessings on the Messenger, the selected one
To him belongs the means of access, even before his selection

So Allāh's blessings on him, so long as purity
Manifests in the stillness of the heart

* * *

O enraptured one: alas for you without the difficulties of the path

You are incomplete; so continue seeking

O seeker: without rapture (jadhb)

You remain veiled, so move and bestir yourself!

The perfected one is he who combines

The two states of rapture and seeking, it is he who progresses with speed

May Allāh include us among such perfected ones

Who have become truly enraptured, but continued traveling the path

...

* * *

Let not the arrived assume leadership,

Until permission is granted; keep the secret concealed

Long silence pleases me:

An indication of gnosis, an informed state

No good is there in expressing (divine realities) at every gathering

Secrets are removed with public mention

May Allāh, Lord of the Throne, care for us, by the secret of His secret

Upon him Allāh's blessing, the disposer of affairs.

Shaykh al-Tijānī is the Sun

The following excerpts are from an early collection of poetry published as "The Collection of Collections" (Jamʿ al-jawāmiʿ).[210] *They concern Shaykh Ibrāhīm's love and respect for the founder of the Tijāniyya Sufi order, Shaykh Aḥmad b. Muḥammad al-Tijānī (d. 1815, Fez).*

* * *

The spiritual support for all gnostics and saints–

In your hands is the purifying and honing of the hearts

And the filling up with cognizance, and secrets and wisdom

I have dismissed contention, so contention of me has been dismissed.

* * *

210 Ibrāhīm Niasse, *Jamʿ al-jawāmiʿ*, 179, 175.

This Shaykh is the sun, and the saintly poles are but stars

The stars are hidden when the sun's brilliance rises

The spiritual support; there is no support other than him, and who is callous

Is but a commander being commanded: he has been eclipsed

The Prophet has become manifest in him, and the Prophet is the manifestation

Of my Lord, Allāh on the throne, to whom belongs devotion

From Shaykh al-Tijānī pours the flood, and the creation is in his fist

For his sake and from him, is obstruction, if he wishes, or provision.

The Bursting Flood

This is an excerpt from the poem, Nafaḥāt al-Malik al-Ghānī,[211] *written during the Shaykh's trip to Guinea in the late 1940s. Most of the following lines were first translated by Andrea Brigaglia in his article, "The Fayḍa Tijaniyya,"*[212] *although the version here represents some changes from Brigaglia's original. Rüdiger Seesemann discussed the poem at length in the book, The Divine Flood.*[213]

* * *

By Bissikrima[214] *I passed during my (outward) journey*

And my return was (with the force) of the Niger River.[215]

There I invoked Him by His greatest name,

---

211 This poem is sometimes referenced also as the *Riḥlat al-Kunākriyya.* The relevant lines here are found in Niasse, *Majmūʿ al-riḥlāt*, 110-111.

212 Andrea Brigaglia, "The Fayḍa Tijaniyya of Ibrāhīm Nyass," *Islam et Sociétés au sud du Sahara*, 14-15 (2000-2001), 54-57.

213 Seesemann, *Divine Flood*, 166-167.

214 A town in central Guinea, situated on a tributary of the Niger river and on the railway line linking Conakry and Kankan.

215 *Nahr Jūlibā*: the word Joliba or "great river" denotes the Niger river in the Mande language.

Drawing near (to Him), myself an offering, burning

And by the invocation, my breast overflowed

Indeed, for it was filled with lights

Lights of essential realities and gnostic understandings,

And the secret of the secret of the secret, and angelic breezes[216]

I carried the secret of the Seal of the Saints,

I combined the knowledge of experience and learning[217]

The tongue of my overflowing spiritual state sang to me

Conversing in the heavenly breaths of the Creator:

"The basin has been filled!" and my body cried,

"Gently! You have stuffed my inside!"

He has bestowed on me special knowledge, and the power of disposition

If I were to say, "Be," it would be, immediately

But from the rules of conduct, I surrendered to Him as Trustee

And so He chose me as His special friend (khalīl)
I said: "There is no god but Allāh,

and Muḥammad has been sent by Allāh."

---

216 The word ʿawārif here is of obscure meaning, seeming to reference the plural of ʿārifa, a synonym (according to Edward Lane's Arabic Lexicon) for an old metaphorical usage of ʿurf, meaning "By the Angels, and the winds, that are sent forth (consecutively like several portions of the horse's mane)."

217 *Dhawq* ("tasting") and *Darāya* ("knowledge") seem to indicate here both an experiential cognizance (*maʿrifa*) and a rational knowledge (ʿilm).

Then from me overflowed His secret, and whoever seeks me with purpose

Attains the knowledge of Allāh, the Eternal Sustainer

The elders the same as the youth

Since the Beloved, the Sanctuary has come close

The men the same as the women

The poor the same as the sultans

Had I wished, this flood of His would have swept the earth

Even the inhabitants of the oceans would have beheld His mysteries

Everyone would have known

But to hear of something, is not the same as to see with the eye

Soon you will see wondrous things

From the flood of this Saintly Seal, Imam of the noble ones

All of this is the flood of (Aḥmad) al-Tijānī

The support (madad) of the chosen of creation, (Muḥammad) al-ʿAdnānī

This is all a favor from (Allāh) the Benefactor

Him I praise secretly and openly

He indeed created me to heal the fracture

For I am the representative of the secret of the secret.[218]

---

218 *Wakīl sirr al-sirr*: in other words, Shaykh Ibrāhīm is the deputy of Shaykh Aḥmad al-Tijānī.

The Rope of Arrival

This poem, "ḥarf yā'" from Awthaq al-'arā fī madḥ sayyid al-warā ("The Most Certain Handhold in Praise of the Master of Creation"),[219] is one of the most frequently recited by students of Shaykh Ibrāhīm Niasse in Senegal.

* * *

May all those who hold to my rope arrive (in the Divine presence)

May he actualize (knowledge), whoever has not given lie to the Lord

And my traversing the deserts of gnosis is beyond (another's) aspiration

So the saintly poles have fallen short in realizing my affair

(This is) by the preference of the Allāh of mankind, mighty and exalted

And (by) the love of the Messenger of Allāh, Ṭā Hā, my Prophet

I swear that no one loves me

219 Niasse, *Dawāwīn al-sitt*, 116-117.

Except the most felicitous, and the opposite for him who hates me

And the people have come to know that I am his servant[220]

So connection to the beloved of Allāh is found in connection to me

And I have not said my words from ecstasy or boasting

And no (spiritual) drunkenness, no departed reason, has touched me

My writings are felicity for the human race

No misery touches him who has seen me or my writing

And I have not said this without authorization, and surely I

In order to conceal a secret, it was not disclosed to other than me

This is from the love of the Master of Messengers

Upon him the blessing of Allāh, (a blessing that) exalts my affair

I have been filled with light from him, until I (myself) was overwhelmed, however

(It was) the majesty of Allāh's Messenger[221] *(that) overwhelmed my thoughts*

His overflowing grace (ifāḍa), love, from Him to Him

So glory to the Lord whose manifestation has annihilated my soul (rūḥ)

And from the secret of this, I died yearning, passionately in love

The closer I came, the more my longing increased

---

220 *Khadīmuhu*: thus servant of the Prophet.

221 *Jalāl Rasūl-Allāḥ*, or "the majesty of Allāh's Messenger" is reference, according to Shaykh Muḥammad al-Māḥī Cissé, to Shaykh Aḥmad al-Tijānī. Muḥammad al-Māhī Cissé, interview with translator, Medina-Baye, Senegal, September, 2008.

So who is for me is for the beloved, and would that I be

His intimate in this life and the next, my (sincere) wish.

Upon him the blessing of Allāh, then peace

Equal to the prayer of (all) the people of remembrance prior to me

Upon him and his noble family and companions (peace)

(Equal to those) who have traveled the open road of love before me.

Illumination in the Cradle

This is an excerpt from "ḥarf hamza" from "The Hermitage of the Lovers" (manāsik ahl al-wadād).[222]

* * *

Every one has his passion, and Ibrāhīm is afflicted
With love of Aḥmad, best of men, the source of all beauty

Only from envy do they wrong me
For since my childhood I have surpassed all peers

My spiritual opening was completed in the cradle, and in the unseen
All the elect have been subdued under my authority

222 Niasse, *al-Dawāwīn al-sitt*, 171-172.

Their convergence from the east and west

On Mecca has been only to smell of my fragrance

Of course: for my essence (ʿayn) today is the essence of Muḥammad

Flowing in me is his secret, from my bones to my comely appearance

The folk of my age have all obtained spiritual elevation

Except those who disdained my path, following their own caprice

Not from intoxication or self-memorial do I say this

All successful folk I have endowed with my protection

By me has the great oppression been lifted[223]

By my flood has the banner of religion been raised.

223 According to Shaykh Ḥasan Cissé (interview with translator, Medina-Baye, 2007), the "oppression" (*jawr*) mentioned here was a reference to the European colonial occupation of Africa.

Never Absent From Me

This is an excerpt from "ḥarf rā'" of "The Cure for Ills" (Shifā' al-asqām).[224]

* * *

My animation is only for the praise of the Prophet, without my boasting

My poetry contains nothing except his praise

Except his praise, all other verse I refuse,

Unless supplication to the Lord or remembrance

Intensely longing for Aḥmad, I return to my Lord

In praising the Prophet, I became exalted above the stars

224 Niasse, *al-Dawāwīn al-sitt*, 159.

Climbed the peak of gnosis, became distinguished in knowledge

Mastered the obscurities of the sciences; and this without boasting

I saw Allāh's Messenger, who generously fulfilled my aspiration

And he has never been absent from me, for all time whether on land or sea

The flag of remembrance and Prophetic praise raised I aloft, while drowning

In the ocean of my beloved, a drowning inspired by his mention.

Shortening the Path

This is an excerpt from "ḥarf zā'" of "The Elixir of Happiness" (Iksīr al-sa'āda).[225]

* * *

I ascended the summit of gnosis ('irfān), passing through all spiritual stations

Until I reached the highest presence, and came to possess the flood

This by love of Allāh's Messenger, Aḥmad my master

So I came to the beloved, and obtained the rewards

225 Niasse, *al-Dawāwīn al-sitt*, 48.

Should the saintly poles be astonished at every unveiling (mashhad)

I took possession of the centers (of meaning) in witnessing the essence of the Divine Essence (ʿayn al-dhāt)

Whatever the distance, I shorten the path for one who loves me

(Arriving) to the exalted Divine presence, though I only point the way

Chapter V

Supplications

Supplication for Cleaning of the Heart

"O Allāh! With You is the Opening" (Allāhumma ʿalayka al-fatḥ)

Shaykh Ibrāhīm mentioned this prayer by name in his early poem, Ruḥ al-adab. Also known by its opening line, "Allāhumma ʿalayka muʿawwalī", the prayer is recited silently after the ritual prayers, and is one of the litanies employed in the process of the aspirant's spiritual education (tarbiya). The prayer is traceable to Shaykh Aḥmad al-Tijānī himself and is also found in some versions of the Tijāniyya's prayer book, Aḥzāb wa awrād.226 In his redaction of the Aḥzāb, Muḥammad al-Ḥafiẓ al-Tijānī (d. 1978, Cairo) wrote that the prayer "is among the remembrances of the Ṭarīqa, for the purpose of connecting the heart with Allāh the Exalted, gathering oneself and returning back to Him; and (for the purpose of) leaving aside everything except for Him, in general matters and in particulars."

* * *

226 Aḥmad al-Tijānī, *Aḥzāb wa awrād*, ed. Muḥammad al-aḤāfiẓ al-Tijānī (Cairo: al-Zāwiya al-Tijaniyya al-Kubrā, 2007), 139–140.

O Allāh! On You is my dependence, and with You is my comfort, and in You is my refuge, and on You is my reliance. With You is my trust, and on Your strength and power is my support. In every occurrence, my contentment is in Your decree. My serenity is in the acknowledgment of the pervasion of Your eternal self-subsistence (*qayyūmiyya*) in each and every thing, and the impossibility of anything, small or large, escaping Your knowledge and Your compulsion for a single moment.

Supplication after Remembrance (wazifa)

This supplication is recited following the congregational remembrance (waẓīfa) by whoever leads it. The prayer consists almost entirely of supplications revealed in the Qur'ān and others made by the Prophet Muḥammad. There are some slight variations in the prayer as it has been recorded in different sources. This translation is based on that found in the Jawahir al-Rasa'il.[227]

* * *

O Allāh! You are the First, and there is nothing before You. You are the Last, and there is nothing after You. You are the Manifest, and nothing can obscure You. You are the Hidden, and nothing can unveil You. O You who are First, Last, Manifest, Hidden; be our Guardian and our Succor. You are our Patron, and what a blessed Patron and Succor You are!

227 Niasse, *Jawāhir al-rasā'il*, II: 84-85.

O Allāh! We ask of You an absolute opening from what has been opened, and a perfect seal from what has been sealed.

O Allāh! We ask of You the good of the present and of what is to come, from what we know and what we do not know. We seek refuge in You from the evil of the present and of what is to come, from what we know and what we do not know.

O Allāh! We ask of You the Garden of Paradise and what comes near to it in word and deed. We seek refuge in You from the Fire of Hell and what comes near to it in word and deed.

O Allāh! We ask of You pardon, well-being, and an unending dispensation (from punishment) in the religion, in the world, and in the hereafter.

O Allāh! We ask of You Your satisfaction, and the satisfaction of Your Prophet, and the satisfaction of our shaykhs, and the satisfaction of our parents.

O Allāh! Make all that we love to be found in what You love, and make Your choice our choice, and allow us to have no exigency except You.

O our Lord! O Creator of all the worlds! Come between us and every wrongdoer, and reward all those who have done good to us with the best reward.

O Allāh! Distance from us hardship, famine and deprivation, and remove from us every affliction, which none can remove except You.

"*Our Lord! Grant us the good of this world and the good of the hereafter, and save us from the punishment of the Fire*".[228]

"*Our Lord! condemn us not if we forget or fall into error. Our Lord! Lay not on us a burden like that laid on those before us.*

---

228 Qur'ān, 2:201.

Our Lord! Charge us not with more than we can bear. Pardon us, forgive us, and have mercy on us. You are our Protector, so grant us victory over the disbelieving people".[229]

"Our Lord! Cause not our hearts to deviate after You have guided us. Bestow on us mercy from Your very presence, indeed, You alone are the One who bestows".[230]

"Our Lord! We have heard the caller calling to faith, (saying) believe in your Lord! So we have believed. Our Lord! Forgive us our sins, and cover up our faults, and allow us to die among the righteous people".[231]

"Our Lord! Grant us what You have promised to Your Messengers, and shame us not on the Day of Resurrection, for You never go back on Your promise".[232]

"Our Lord! We have wronged our own selves, and if You do not forgive us and have mercy on us, we will surely be among the lost ones".[233]

"Our Lord! Grant us mercy from Your very presence, and assure for us guidance in our affairs".[234]

"Our Lord! Bestow on us spouses and offspring that are the light of our eyes, and grant us (the grace) to lead the pious".[235]

O Allāh! forgive our living and our dead, our adults and our children, our men and our women, our freemen and our servants, those of us present and those of us absent, the obedient ones among us and the disobedient.

---

229 Qur᾽ān, 2:286.
230 Qur᾽ān, 3:8.
231 Qur᾽ān, 3:193.
232 Qur᾽ān, 3:194.
233 Qur᾽ān, 7:23.
234 Qur᾽ān, 18:10.
235 Qur᾽ān, 25:74.

O Allāh! Send Your blessing upon our master Muḥammad, who opened what was closed, who sealed what preceded him; who aided the truth by the truth, the guide to Your straight path. And upon his family (as well), may this (prayer) be deserving of his worth, for indeed his worth is exceedingly great.

"*Glory to your Lord, the Lord of honor and power, (exalted) is He above what they ascribe to Him. And peace upon the Messengers. All praise is due to Allāh, Lord of all the worlds*".[236]

---

236 Qur'ān, 37:180-182.

“The subjection of the horizons in the prayer on the master of Buraq.”

Taskhīr al-afāq fī ṣalāt ʿalā ṣāḥib al-Burāq

Kanz al-Maṣūn, p. 63-72

This supplication was written in the 1930s and originally included near the end of the cherished manuscript Sirr al-akbar (“The Greatest Secret”). It was printed in the 2007 publication of Kanz al-maṣūn, Shaykh Ḥasan Cissé’s collection of Shaykh Ibrāhīm’s supplications.[237] *The supplication is based on the well-known Tijānī prayer, Jawharat al-kamāl (“The Jewel of Perfection”), to be recited before the supplication itself. The Jawharat al-kamāl is translated first, followed by the supplication.*

* * *

237 Ibrāhīm Niasse, *Kanz al-maṣūn*, 63-72.

O Allāh! Send blessings and peace on the eye of Divine mercy; the true ruby; the guarded enclosure, encompassing the center of understandings and meanings;

The light of creation, the Adamic being, the possessor of Divine Truth; The most brilliant flash of lightning in the profitable rain clouds which fills all the intervening seas and receptacles; Your bright light with which You have filled Your universe, encompassing all places of existence.

O Allāh! Send blessings and peace on the eye of the Real, from whom are manifested the thrones of realities; the source of the most precious gnosis; Your complete, most straight path.

O Allāh! Send blessings and peace on the manifestation of Truth by the truth, the greatest treasure; Your overflowing profusion, from You and (returning) to You, the encompassment of esoteric light; Allāh's blessing on him and his family; a prayer which we come to know him.

* * *

In the Name of Allāh, the Compassionate the Merciful.

"**O Allāh! Bless and salute the eye of Divine Mercy**," a prayer from the presence of Compassion, accompanied by the spirit of Lordship. By this prayer, drown me in the ocean of compassion, and let flow upon me in every instant sixty-six million floods (*fayda*) from among the floods of Divine Compassion. Give me in each flood the most abundant good fortune and ample share of every goodness, whether of this world or the next, which has ever been asked You by our master Muḥammad, may Allāh's blessing and peace be upon him.

"**A True Ruby**," and allow this scintillating ruby to take possession of my heart, so that by it I come to actualize the Greatest Name and Its Secret. Illuminate my heart until it shines, so that by this ruby I see the unseen worlds of the universe, until neither the unseen external worlds nor the subtleties of the hidden worlds are hidden from me. By this ruby let me see the perfection of Your Essence (*dhāt*).

"**The Guarded Enclosure**," so guard me by this from the entirety of existence in whatever way You will, and subject for us by it the whole of existence, in both its totality and particulars. And by this enclosure take hold for me of the souls (*arwāh*), the forelocks, the hearts and the feet, until I have complete power of disposal in the universe, the disposal of the greatest of gnostics, those perfected and completed, the saintly poles and spiritually elevated. And by this enclosure put their forelocks in my hand, and turn them with Your permission where I will, and allow my disposal to be in them as I want. Subject for me their hearts to love me, love accompanied by longing and awe, by the secret of Divine Mercy and its eye (*'ayn*), by the ruby and its essence, indeed You have power over all things.

"**Encompassing the Center of Understandings and Meanings**." Make the world (*dunya*) a place of establishment for me, a riding animal at my obedience and command, that I move through it with your permission where I will and how I will; that I have power of disposition in it with what You love, and that You are pleased with it (my disposition) tangibly and abstractly, (that this is bestowed) with tranquility, forgiveness and well-being from every sort of affliction. (May Your pleasure) be unlimited, so long as eternity should last, indeed You have power over all things, and You are capable of response, *amīn*, *amīn*.

"**The Light of Creation, the Adamic Being, the Possessor of Divine Truth**." O Allāh, I ask you by this perfection of Your Light, and perfection of Your Essential Being, a light that transforms my body, allowing it to become pure luminosity. By him make my heart a glittering jewel, an unblemished pearl, a brilliant, illuminated ruby; a polished, truthful mirror, in companionship with You openly and secretly, until I do not perceive except in You, and I do not hear except from You, and I do not move except by You, and I do not rest except in You; that I witness the oneness (*waḥda*) in the unseen world (as) the uniqueness of Your Countenance (*wajh*), and the multiplicity in the external world (as) a reality of Your essential Oneness. (May the Prophet be) a light that fills my heart with certainty, and establishes me in the degrees of the Greatest Name, and in the hidden realm of his comprehensive and exalted secret, until I am in the station of extinguishment (*saḥq*) and eradication (*maḥq*), and (in the station of) gathering of the gathering: (both) collected and dispersed, erased and confirmed, intoxicated but with perfect sobriety. By this (Adamic Being of the Prophet) assist me – in the beautiful way of beauty – with the perfected jewel (*al-jawhara al-kāmila*), the pearl, the lustrous scintillating ruby, with the perfection of the light of the immaculate, unique pearl; a mighty support that strengthens me, helps me, gives me victory, protects me, and conquers our enemies and the enviers, and subject for me the entirety of creation, wholly and individually, through sufficiency from them. And assist me with good offspring, full of blessing; and with a wide provision, full of blessing; and with a long life full of goodness and obedience; and with a beautiful covering (*sitr*) in the religion, in the world, and in the afterlife. And (assist me with) righteous wives, and make them the delight of my eyes. Let me not see in them (my household) anything except that which delights the eye, and let me not hear from them anything except that which pleases the ear, literally and metaphorically, secretly and openly. Subject to me the creation. Let them serve me by Your pervasive authorization, secreted in every one of them. Put them in my hand, under my decision, and make them compelled in obedience to me, subdued, and compliant by the greatness of my awe-inspiring presence (*hayba*) and the mightiness of my power in them. And let this be by the awe, majesty, and exaltedness of Allāh, and let it be joined with security, pardon, success, and well-being forever and ever,

Amen. O Lord, surely You have power over all things, and are worthy of answering (this prayer). And may Allāh's blessing be on our master Muḥammad, and on his family: (a prayer) worthy of his merit, and his worth is exceedingly great.

O Allāh, send blessings and peace on "**the most brilliant flash of lightning in the profitable rain clouds which fill all the intervening seas and receptacles**." A prayer by which You flash upon us the lightning flashes of the grand illumination (*al-fatḥ al-akbar*), until our hearts are opened: an opening in reality, lightning flashes that You make manifest in our hearts in brilliant radiance, that You make shine therein with luster, that You light therein with luminosity. By this (illumination) we witness the perfection of Your Essence (*dhāt*), and we realize Your exaltedness and greatness, and we become distinguished, the elite of the elite. O Lord! Cause this jewel to become established in our hearts with sincerity and permanence. By this (illumination) flood our hearts with the overflowing floods of knowledge, gnosis, lights, illuminations, endowments, authorities, realities, and rare gifts. That we may benefit from the full rain clouds in our hearts, a felicitous benefit of the two eternal abodes, that we may stand in your presence in true worship, exposing ourselves to beneficial rainclouds filling the presence of the seas of Prophecy and the receptacles of sainthood, always, forever, in safety, amnesty, and well-being. Amen. May Allāh bless our master Muḥammad, (a prayer) worthy of his merit, and his worth is exceedingly great.

O Allāh send blessings and peace on "**Your bright light with which You have filled Your universe, encompassing all places of existence**." A prayer by which You illuminate our innermost beings (*asrār*), our souls (*arwāḥ*), our intellects, and our hearts. (A prayer by which) You purify our carnal selves (*anfus*): a perfect, utmost, and complete purification. (A prayer by which) You clean our bodies (*ajsām*) in perfect purification, (by which) you train our beings (*ajsād*) with a complete refinement, by which You grant Your subtle grace so that we attain to the highest purification. A prayer by which You envelop us in the essence of the absolute (*huwiya al-muṭlaq*), an enveloping that removes from us the five senses, until we do not feel anything, we do not know anything, we are not aware of anything, do not think of anything, we do not see anything, we do not hear anything, and we do not sense anything except the Truth (*al-Ḥaqq*), by the Truth, in the Truth, about the Truth, for the Truth, on the Truth, from the Truth. O Allāh, cause Your brilliant light to fill our hearts, a light which becomes a spirit (*rūḥ*) to us, by which we encompass the universe, in all the places of existence. Make us a perfect human being (*insān kāmil*), an Adamic being of (Angelic) spirits, of (Divine) attributes and names; and this with safety, pardon, and well-being forever and eternally. Amen. And may Allāh's blessing be on our master Muḥammad, and on the people of our master Muḥammad, a prayer worthy of his merit, and surely his worth is exceedingly great.

"**O Allāh, send blessings and peace on the eye of the Real, from whom are manifested the thrones of realities; the source of the most precious gnosis; Your complete, most straight path.**" A prayer by the Name of the degree of the Divine Essence upon the eye of the Essence (ʿayn al-dhāt); a prayer by which You pour upon us floods from the treasuries of compassion; by which You open for us the treasuries of Divine grace. A prayer by which you pour upon us the flood of the Saintly Seal (Aḥmad) al-Tijānī; by which You rain upon us, O Allāh, O Compassionate, from the clouds of provision every manner of wealth. And this with ease and facility, by Your grace and Your compassion. Surely You have power over all things, and are worthy of the response.

O Allāh, make the truth our companion, our character, our intimacy, our beloved, our consultation, our dear friend. Make us the beloved ones, the loving ones, the saved ones, the sincere ones, the most truthful ones, the ones brought close, the ones granted certainty, the illuminated ones — (those granted) the greatest illumination (*al-fatḥ al-akbar*), the illumination in certainty, the illumination soon in coming, from every door among the doors of Your compassion. Make us the ones helped, the ones assisted, the ones victorious; this by the secret of the "Jewel of Perfection", and the Infinite Divine Identity (*al-huwiyya*). *Amīn*. May Allāh's blessing be upon our master Muḥammad, and on his family, worthy of his merit, and surely his worth is exceedingly great.

"O Allāh, send blessings and peace on the manifestation of Truth by the truth, the greatest treasure." A prayer by which we are granted insight into the Presence of the Absolute; by which we come to actualize the Prophetic realities, the presence of "worthy of his merit" (*ḥaqq qadrihi*). (A prayer by which) we are extinguished in the bountiful presence of the Hidden Pole (*quṭb al-maktūm*), the sphere of the sealed enclosure; and (by which) we come to abide within the presence of "his worth is exceedingly great" (*miqdarihi l-ʿaẓīm*), coming to perceive the greatest treasure. (Make our) erasure a true reality, and (make our) establishment (in the world) a passage (to the next world). (Grant us) beauty within beauty, annihilation with abiding, intoxication with sobriety. Make us those who uphold the religion; those on the path of Muḥammad (*al-Muḥammadiyyīn*), in submission (*islām*), faith (īmān), and excellence (*iḥsān*); those who uphold the law (*al-ḥudūd*) secretly and openly.

O Allāh, grant us realization by Your compassion, and compel us by Your grace. Grant us victory and assistance over all of our enemies and enviers. Make between them and us a preventative protection, a walled veil: impenetrable to piercing lances and violent storms. Open for us the countries (*bilād*), the villages and the cities. Open for us the locked doors, whether in the religion, in the world, or the afterlife. Subject completely to us the entirely of the creation. Make us wealthy, but sufficient from them, in security and wellbeing. May Allāh's blessing be upon our master Mu*h*ammad, a prayer worthy of his merit, and surely his worth is exceedingly great.

O Allāh, send blessings and peace upon "**Your overflowing profusion, from You and (returning) to You, the encompassment of esoteric light; Allāh's blessing on him and his family; a prayer which we come to know him**." By this prayer pour upon us the lights of the perfection of the Divine Essential Being. Let us be in the presence of "worthy of his merit, and his worth is exceedingly great;" (an existence) from You, to You, in You, and with You. Take us (back to You) gently. Elevate us to highest stations of the spiritually elite; the elite of the elite; in the presence of the (saintly) Seal, the finishing point of the most distinguished among the exalted elite. Make Your hidden, subtle, delicate light the light of our vision, the healing of our hearts, the strength of our souls, the cure of our sicknesses, the luminosity of our minds, and the secret of our remembrance, of our delight, of our refuge, of our resting. (Make this light) our protector, our helper, our beloved, our dear friend, our companion, our succor, our assistance. Grant us the power of disposition in all things. Attract to us all good, and subject to us every single person, and give us victory over everyone, and protect us from everyone. Make us sufficient from every thing that attracts our attention, and from that which escapes our attention, in the religion, in the world, and in the afterlife. Pour upon us sufficiency in the two abodes (of this life and the next). Cover us in the covering of beauty. Put the forelocks, the feet, the hearts, and the souls of the creation in our hands. Give us a good, long life, filled with blessing and obedience. Facilitate for us provision, and wealth in gold, silver, livestock, money, and servants. And give us blessing in all of this. Provide us with righteous spouses: well covered, devout, virtuous, upstanding, fertile, submissive (to Allāh), faithful, obedient, patient, strong in effort, and knowledgeable (of the Real). And grant us plentiful, good offspring full of blessing.

O Allāh, place this light in our hearts so that we may gain proximity to You, so that we become beloved to You. Make us sincere and protect us. Unveil for us all of the unseen things of the creation, and give us insight into the creation, a true and ocular insight. Allow us to penetrate the veils, and take away from us deficiencies. Bring light to us in darkness. Drive doubt away from us. Give us inspiration in all things among the creation. Unveil for us the reality of all things among the unseen affairs, both in wakefulness and dream, both while traveling and at home. Teach us about everything: knowledge of the earlier generations and the later ones. Give us power over the tyrants, the sultans, the princes, and the righteous saints; a true sovereignty both among the black and red (beings). Raise our degrees in the religion, in the world, and in the afterlife. Be for us a protector and a helper. O Lord, do not leave for us any need except that it be answered more swiftly than the blinking of an eye; whether small or large, manifest or hidden, secret or public; whether pertaining to the religion, the world, or the afterlife. And this by Your grace and mercy, O most merciful of the merciful. *Amīn*. And may Allāh's blessing on our master Muḥammad, a prayer worthy of his merit, and surely his merit is exceedingly great.

Chapter VI

Spiritual Witnessing

Witnessing the Divine Presence

The Mashhad of Shaykh Ibrāhīm Niasse

The following excerpt, from some of Shaykh Ibrāhīm's unpublished writings, was included in Imam Shaykh al-Tijānī Cissé's 2011 speech in Ivory Coast, "Mā qālahu al-ʿārifūn bi-Llāh ʿan al-maʿrifa bi-Llāh." This remarkable speech later appeared in Shaykh al-Tijānī's book of compiled speeches, Knowing Allāh, Living Islam.[238]

* * *

A momentous occurrence happened to the humble servant writing this in the year 1350 after the Hijra of Muḥammad, upon him blessing and peace. It was this: I came to abide (*makathtu*) for a hundred thousand years among the days of the Lord. There I heard the purest, pre-eternal speech in intimate conversation. I became bewildered and restless, as both rapture and aching were joined in me.

---

238 Shaykh al-Tijānī Cissé, *Knowing Allāh, Living Islam* (trans. Zachary Wright, Ibrāhīm Naseem, Muḥammad Hassiem Tijani; Singapore: Light of Eminence, 2014), 74-76.

Then I plunged headlong into the Divine Presence, and I witnessed there the reality of the reality of the reality of the reality, in utter essentiality, exclusivity, and blind effacement. Nothing was left of sensory feelings. I dwelled like this for two hundred thousand years.

Then something was with me. The existence emerged from me like shadows or smoke. And I sought after this existence, and then I was with the Messenger, from the Divine Essential Being (*dhāt*), the servant of the Divine Essential Being and Its secret. And he came close to me and stayed suspended until I disappeared in him. He became my essence. Then I was overcome with joy, for I was the beloved of the Divine Essential Being, Its secret, Its servant, Its desire. I was that which held Its comprehensive station (*martabatahā al-jāmiʿa*), to whom the perfection of the Divine Essential Being was manifest. I resided in my state of rapture for one million years.

In this manifestation in the unseen (*ghayb*), I did not find any servant of the Divine Essential Being except myself. But then there was another manifestation, unseen out of the unseen, and I saw a majestic awe (*jalāl*) in the ultimate beauty (*jamāl*). In this presence of the unseen of the unseen, I was called forth and named, "O Aḥmad al-Tijānī!" I knew for certain that the Real had no desire for anything, after the secret, except for me. I kept company with this servant of the Divine Essential Being, and I helped him and aided him for two million years.

Then Allāh made me the father of humanity (*abū l-bashar*), and the spiritual support (*madad*) for the entirety of existent beings, the Adam of souls and spirits. I carried the trust (*amāna*), and I was called to, "*O Dāwūd, surely We have made you the khalīfa on the earth.*"[239] I looked at the earth, and saw its state, the worlds of sense and of meaning, and then the celes-

239 Qurʾān, 38:26.

tial gathering, and the lower gathering. "*We built the heaven with might, and We it is who made the vast expanse. And We have laid out the earth. Gracious is He who spread it out! And all things We have created in pairs, that haply you may reflect. Therefore flee to Allāh. I am a warner to you from Him. Set up no other gods besides Allāh. I am a warner to you from Him.*"[240] So I came back to my sensory feeling, and it was if the time period of the occurrence was between the even and the odd. Glory to Allāh the Majestic. He selects whom He wills for what He wills, and no one outstrips His wisdom. "*And He is not asked about what He does, but they are the ones asked.*"[241]

240 Qurʾān, 51:47-51.
241 Qurʾān, 21:23.

Appendix

"Shaykh Ibrāhīm Niasse: Revivalist of the Sunnah"

By Shaykh Ḥasan Cissé

Shaykh Ibrāhīm Niasse: Revivalist of the Sunnah

by Shaykh Ḥasan Ali Cissé

Shaykh Ḥasan Cissé first presented this paper at the Conference on Islam in Africa: the Changing Role of the Ulama, hosted by the Program of African Studies at Northwestern University (Evanston, IL), March 28-31, 1984. It was later published the same year by the Ṭarīqa Tijāniyya of New York. It remains one of the most succinct and useful expositions of Shaykh Ibrāhīm's life and work. The version presented here has been edited slightly, mostly in the form of a few added footnotes to provide background to Shaykh Ḥasan's discussion and to present some corroborating sources published since the 1984 presentation of the paper.

* * *

Shaykh al-Islām al-Ḥājj Ibrāhīm Niasse was truly an ocean without shore, blessed by Allāh with numerous gifts, good deeds, and noble character traits. But if we were limited to describing the Shaykh in one word, we would definitely describe him simply as a Muslim – somebody who gave his life for the sake of Islam in every time, place, and situation. As a Muslim, he did his best to follow the footsteps of the Prophet Muḥammad, may the peace and blessings of Allāh be upon him. He wrote in one poem, "If I am asked, 'What is your path (*madhhab*), and who is your beloved?' I will surely answer, 'It is the Prophet.'"

Shaykh Ibrāhīm was born in Senegal on October 17, 1902 (15 Rajab, 1320 A.H.) and died on July 26, 1975 (15 Rajab 1395 A.H.). He was the son of alḤājj ʿAbd-Allāh Niasse and the grandson of Muḥammad Niasse, both well-known Islamic scholars of the Senegambia region. Growing up in an intellectual environment only strengthened his grasp of the Islamic sciences. His father taught him Qurʾān and its exegesis (*tafsīr*) as well as Ḥadīth and their explanations (*sharḥ*). He also taught him jurisprudence (*fiqh*) and the science of Sufism (*taṣawwuf*) from the well-known books in use among the *majālis al-ʿilm*, those circles in which students seeking knowledge gather around the shaykhs.

As a boy, the Shaykh was highly intelligent and blessed with good character and potential. These characteristics once prompted his father to say, "You do not need to travel as your brothers do. If you but sit, people will come to you. It is the duty of a river to be full. If the neighboring cows do not come to drink, those who are from afar will." In reference to his educational background and achievements, Shaykh Ibrāhīm said, "I learned Qurʾān and Ḥadīth first from my shaykh, my father, and he, from his father. I received an ʿijāza (traditional license to teach) first from my father in both Qurʾān and Ḥadīth, then from ʿAbd al-Raḥmān b. al-Ḥājj al-ʿAlawī and another *ʿijāza* from Shaykh Aḥmad Sukayrij who, himself, had earned some six hundred *ʿijāza*s from six hundred different shaykhs whose names are mentioned in his book where he writes, 'The first one to whom I gave authorization in all these chains of transmission was the Khalīfa al-Ḥājj Ibrāhīm Niasse.'"[242]

When Shaykh Ibrāhīm entered upon the Sufi path, he took the Ṭarīqa Tijāniyya from his father. The step was momentous, for it was within this Ṭarīqa that he was to play a major role. It was, in fact, a role without parallel since Shaykh ʿUmar Tāl al-Fūtī's earlier role in the spread of the Tijāniyya.[243]

Starting with his father, Shaykh Ibrāhīm received many appointments as propagator (*muqaddam*) of the Tijāniyya. Before dying, his father instructed Shaykh Muḥammad Mahmoud al-Shinqītī of Mauritania to appoint his son a muqaddam. Shaykh ash-Shinjity, however, told Shaykh Ibrāhīm, "You have no need for an *ʿijāza* from a creature because you have your appointment from the Creator."[244] He had additional appointments from al-Ḥājj ʿAbd-Allāh b. al-Ḥājj al-ʿAlawī of Mauritania and the master Muḥammad al-Ḥāfiẓ al-Tijānī of Egypt as well as Shaykh Aḥmad Sukayrij of Morocco, the closest link to Shaykh Aḥmad Tijānī in the chain of initiatory transmission (*silsila*).[245] He certified that Shaykh Ibrāhīm was the inheritor (*khalīfa*) of Shaykh Aḥmad Tijānī.

---

242 Aḥmad Sukayrij, *Qadam al-rusūkh fimā li-muʾallifihi min al-shuyūkh* (unpublished manuscript, copy in library of Shaykh Ḥasan Cissé, Medina-Kaolack, Senegal). See also, Zachary Wright, *Living Knowledge in West African Islam: the Sufi Community of Ibrāhīm Niasse* (Leiden: Brill, 2015), 196.

243 al-Ḥājj ʿUmar al-Futi Tal (d. 1864), prominent Fulani scholar and jihadist. He composed the *Kitab al-Rimah*, one of the most comprehensive and scholarly works published in the nineteenth century throughout the Muslim world, described by John Hunwick as "a contribution to Islamic intellectual history" (Hunwick, "An Introduction to the Tijānī Path" in *Islam et Societes au sud du sahara* (1973), 21). Al-Ḥājj ʿUmar also briefly established a Muslim caliphate in western Mali and eastern Senegal, but was killed fighting combined French and Bambara forces.

244 Shaykh Ibrāhīm Niasse, *Kāshif al-ilbās* (Cairo, 2001), 158.

245 Shaykh Ibrāhīm's most significant *silsila*, or "golden chain", thus became: the Prophet Muḥammad to Shaykh Aḥmad Tijānī to Sidi ʿAlī

Shaykh Ibrāhīm once said, "What I have in the way of ʿijāza and *muqaddam* authorizations would indeed fill a book." Although he was the youngest of his father's children, he became the most outstanding among them. In fact, shortly after his father's death in 1922, he became the most important *marabout* [shaykh] both within his father's house and throughout the area. His importance is reflected in *Notes et Études sur l'Islam en Afrique Noir* where we find the statement, "Al-Ḥājj Ibrāhīm Niasse is indisputably the most remarkable religious personality of the Senegalese Tijaniyya in the Sine-Saloum region and of the Niasse scholarly family."[246] For the first time since the Ṭarīqa's founder, Shaykh Aḥmad Tijānī, there was once again found an international Muslim following.

Shaykh Ibrāhīm was thus blessed with a special charisma for his mission. It should not surprise us, therefore, that this advent was foretold not only by Shaykh Aḥmad Tijānī, but also by Uthman Dan Fodio (d. 1817). Shaykh Aḥmad Tijānī predicted, "A flood (*fayḍa*), will overwhelm my companions to the point that people will enter our path in multitudes. This *fayḍa* will come at a time when mankind will be in a state of utmost difficulties."[247] Shakyh Ibrāhīm began his mission in 1929 – the year of the beginning of the Great Depression. Prior to Shaykh Ibrāhīm, there were many claimants to the possession of the *fayḍa*, yet, in none of them is the characteristic so well reflected as it is in Shaykh Ibrāhīm. The fact that Shaykh Ibrāhīm was indeed the owner of the *fayḍa* has been acknowledged and corroborated by many prominent Tijānī leaders.

There is a parable that Professor Ibrāhīm Mahmud Diop heard from Shaykh Ibrāhīm which helps to explain the concept of *fayḍa*. We are to picture five things. First, imagine a

---

al-Tamasani to Aḥmad ʿAbdalāwī to Aḥmad Sukayrij to Shaykh Ibrāhīm.

246 Marcel Chailley, *Notes et Études sur l'Islam en Afrique Noire* (Paris: Peyronnet, 1962), 143.

247 Muḥammad al-Ṭayyib al-Sufyānī, *Ifādat al-Aḥmadiyya li murīd al-sa'āda wa al-ʿabdiyya* (Cairo, 1971).

fathomless well – not an ordinary well, but a well which has no bottom. Next, imagine a tireless worker who continually draws water from that well. Then imagine a leather bucket that never needs repair. Fourthly, imagine a basin next to that well which eventually becomes full. Finally, imagine water so precious it cannot be thrown away and yet cannot be put back into the well already over-flowing. The question arises, what should be done with the water after the basin is full? The answer: many basins will be constructed around the well to receive the precious water. In the parable, the well represents Allāh, glorified and exalted is He, whose being is continuous without end. The water is Divine gnosis (*ma ʿrifa*) and experience (*dhawq*). The leather bucket is the Prophet. A saying among the Sufis indicates, "Without an intermediary one never reaches a goal and the Prophet is the greatest intermediary between the creation and Allāh." The worker in the parable is Shaykh Aḥmad Tijānī. The basin is an extraordinary spiritual adept who has received so much in the way of Divine Gnosis that he must communicate this Gnosis to others or it will overflow. He is the owner of the *fayḍa* or flood – Shaykh Ibrāhīm Niasse.

In the book *Kanz al-awlād*, Muḥammad Sambu b. Aḥmad (d. 1832) mentioned that Shaykh Uthman Dan Fodio [ʿUthmān b. Fūdī] had prophesied that many members of the scholarly community (ʿulamāʾ), and men distinguished by saintliness, would follow a certain Shaykh Ibrāhīm. In the beginning of a poem written in Fulani, Shaykh Uthman Dan Fodio mentioned the excellences of the ʿulamāʾ both in his time and in the time to come.[248] Among those whom he cited stands the name of a Shaykh Ibrāhīm, along with a description of his character: "His name is Ibrāhīm, his inward name is 'Honor of the Religion' (*Sharaf al-Din*), for the religion of Islam will be honored in his time." He also wrote, "He will come from the

248 The original publication of Shaykh Ḥasan's speech included ʿUthman b. Fūdī's poem in Fulani.

west[249] and will appear in Hausa-land in the year 1370[250] after the Hijra." In another ten verses his face is described as being wide with large eyes. His build is described and it is said that he will be a frequent visitor to the sacred precincts of Mecca and Medina. Finally, it is said that after his appearance there will be a resurgence in the affairs of the Muslims and all shall be under his domain. This Shaykh Ibrāhīm will gather the scattered and bring them together in unity. Shaykh Uthman also mentioned Shaykh Ibrāhīm's father ʿAbd-Allāh by name.

Shaykh Uthman was correct in his timing. It was in that year that Shaykh Ibrāhīm Niasse made a very popular second visit to Hausa-land. The shaykhs, the scholars, and the people came out in masses to renew their affiliation to Islam and the Ṭarīqa. His first visit to Hausa-land, in 1945, was limited to the Amir of Kano, ʿAbd-Allāhi Bayero. But on this second visit, the people showered him with affection in such a loving way that Shaykh Ibrāhīm wrote in one poem:

> *When I arrived there, I was amazed to see what I saw. It was, I swear, beyond whatever I could imagine. My confidence in Allāh's rule of things just as He wills was thus confirmed. I said then, "Where is this Shaykh to whom the necks of the great men stretch forth to greet? Where is this Ibrāhīm, and who is he that they should be so consumed in love for him?" I swear, had I not immersed myself in the love of Shaykh Aḥmad Tijani, surely my very life would have expired from shame.*[251]

The reception that the Shaykh received was such that a prominent Hausa scholar said in a poem:

---

249 Senegal is indeed to the west of Nigeria.

250 This number was apparently referred to cryptically with certain letters, the numerological equivalent of which was 1370 A.H. (1950/1951 C.E.).

251 Shaykh Ibrāhīm Niasse, *Nayl al-Mufazir bi al-Awdi ila al-Hijaz.*

The greatest proof that Shaykh Ibrāhīm is the right person is that the Hausa of Kano, Katsina Zaria, and Bornu submit to him. In that alone is evidence for a righteous person to believe in him. Return then to Kumasi and see Accra, and go up to Lagos, let alone Ilorin and Bida, not to mention Okene. Look there at the folk of Adamawa, Bauchi and Gombe; go then up to Sokoto and Gondo. Even in Sokoto [a centre of the Qadariyya], so folk follow him. Look now at the happy reception at his landing in Kano, where a gathering of the cities walked in multitudes to greet him. He went to Mecca. Happy were they at his arrival. He went then to Medina, whose folk also accepted his leadership. The magnates and shaykhs all came to him and acknowledged that, in him, they had found a true spiritual master of the worlds.[252]

Shaykh Ibrāhīm enjoyed such wide acceptance as a leader among the Tijanis that the Mauritanian Arabs who had first brought the Tijānī Ṭarīqa to Senegal came back in order to renew their *silsilas* with him.[253] They followed him in his movement of return to the Prophet's Sunnah and in uniting the Tijāniyya. Although his father joined the Ṭarīqa in 1875, it came to pass that the Shaykh, his son, became the highest-ranking Tijānī. One can truly say that Shaykh Ibrāhīm Niasse was the Uthman Dan Fodio of his time. Indeed, his message was so full of truth that many of his followers believed him to be the Renewer (*mujaddid*) of his age.[254]

---

252 This in a poem by Malam Balaby. The original printing contains the relevant verses in Hausa script.

253 For more on this subject, see Diana Stone, "The inversion of a historical tendency? The Tijaniyya Niass movement in Mauritania" (paper presented at University of Illinois symposium, "Tijaniyya traditions and societies in West Africa in the 19th and 20th centuries," April 1-5, 1996.

254 In a Ḥadīth related in Imam Aḥmad Ḥanbal's Musnad, on the authority of Abu Hurayra, the Prophet Muḥammad told his followers that a Renewer of Islam would come once every century.

Although Uthman Dan Fodio had fought a jihad of the sword, the jihad of Shaykh Ibrāhīm was fought with speeches, prayers, and the pen. In many ways, the age in which he lived required this form of jihad. He was able to retain communication with his followers all over the world – throughout the African continent, in parts of Asia, and in both the Near and Far East. In Africa alone his followers were counted in the millions. The nature of the movement he initiated is such that, even since the Shaykh's death, it is still gathering followers on the American continent and other places that the Shaykh himself never visited.

The content of his message was concerned with the Sunnah of the Prophet and its revitalization. His goal was to revitalize the Sunnah, in which he lived and embraced. It could scarcely have been otherwise. For throughout his life, the model and path of the Prophet was his model and path. Once I heard the Shaykh say, "If the best of mankind, the Prophet, is moving, even I shall follow him step by step; and the day he stops, from there I shall never move."

Shaykh Ibrāhīm was a staunch advocate of restoring the proper ritual observances of the Prophet's pure Sunnah. Much of his effort in issues of jurisprudence (*fiqh*) was directed at restoring the proper observance of the prayer (*ṣalāt*), reminding Muslims that prayer was the basis of the religion, and encouraging them to perform their prayers in the proper times. Based on the Prophetic tradition, "Pray in the way you see me pray," the Shaykh focused his efforts on what he considered the most frequent omissions from the prayer in Africa at the time. These included the practice of placing the hands on the breast while standing in prayer (*qabḍ*);[255] reciting the opening

255 Traditional Mālikī practice in North and West Africa was to pray with the hands hanging at the sides of the body. For Shaykh Ibrāhīm's discussion of the Ḥadīth calling for *qabḍ*, see Niasse, *Raf' al-malām'an man rafa'a wa qabada iqtidā'an bi sayyid al-anām* ("The removal of blame from who raises his hands and places them on the chest while praying in imitation of

"In the Name of Allāh the Compassionate the Merciful" out loud (when the prayer is to be said out loud) before the *Fātiha*;[256] and raising the hands before and after bowing (*rukū* ʿ).[257] In his primary work treating issues of jurisprudence, *Rafʿ al-malām ʿan man rafaʿa wa qabada iqtidāʾan bi sayyid al-anām*, the Shaykh rejects the notion of the closing of the gates of scholarly reasoning (*ijtihād*).[258]

---

the best of mankind", published by Ibrāhīm ibn Maʾmun b. Ibrāhīm Niasse, unknown place and date of publication), 51-69. As indicated by the title, the Shaykh's aim seems to have been to remove the "blame" on those who prayed *qabḍ,* not to force Mālikīs to abandon *sadl.* In any case, Shaykh Ibrāhīm Niasse was not the only Mālikī scholar to argue for *qabḍ.* For more discussion of this issue, see Wright, *Living Knowledge in West African Islam,* 224-228.

256 This was a practice instituted by Shaykh Aḥmad Tijānī himself, but which most other members of the Mālikī school in North and West Africa do not practice.

257 This based on the Ḥadīth, "Everything has its beauty and the beauty of *ṣalāt* is the raising of the hands."

258 In fact, the gates of *ijtihād* were never actually closed, but continued within the juristic schools, as Shaykh Ibrāhīm's argument here actually demonstrates. See Wael Hallaq, "Was the Gate of Ijtihad Closed?" (*International Journal of Middle East Studies,* 16, 1 (1984): 3-41). Shaykh Ibrāhīm's notion of *ijtihād* seems to closely parallel that expressed by a widespread scholarly network emerging in the eighteenth century, including the likes of Ibrāhīm al-Kurani (d. 1689), Abd al-Ghani al-Nabulsi (d. 1731), al-Ujaymi, Shah Wali Allāh, Abd al-Aziz al-Dabbagh, Mustafa al-Bakri, Muḥammad al-Hifni, Mir Dard, Muḥammad Hayat al-Sindi, Aḥmad Tijani, Aḥmad ibn Idris and Muḥammad al-Sanusi. For more on eighteenth-century scholarly networks, see Bernd Radtke, "Sufism in the 18th Century: an attempt at a provisional appraisal," in *Die Welt des Islam* (36, 3, 1996); Radtke, "Ijtihad and Neo-Sufism", in *Asiatische Studien* (19, 3, 1994); Knut Vikor, "The Development of Ijtihad and Islamic Reform, 1750-1850", paper presented at the *Nordic Conference on Middle Eastern Studies* (Joensuu, Finland, June 19-22, 1995); John Voll, "Muḥammad Hayya al-Sindi and Muḥammad ibn Abd al-Wahhab: an analysis of an intellectual group in eighteenth-century Medina", in Bulletin of the School of Oriental and African Studies (38, 1, 1975); Rudolph Peters, "Idjtihad and Taqlid in 18th and 19th Century Islam," in *Die Welt des Islam* (20, 3/4, 1980); B.M. Nafi, "Taṣawwuf and Reform in pre-modern Islamic Culture: in search of Ibrāhīm al-Kurani", in *Die Welt des Islam* (42, 3, 2002).

As with other reformers, the changes advocated by Shaykh Ibrāhīm caused quite a stir in many communities who remained attached to what they perceived to be authentic Mālikī practice, practices confirmed in their eyes simply by being passed from one generation to the next. But in time, a large segment of the Muslim population throughout West Africa followed the revitalized practice of the Sunnah, championed by Shaykh Ibrāhīm. This event, in particular the practice of praying publicly with the hands crossed on the chest, was the beginning of the "Reformed Tijaniyya" as it has been called in John Paden's excellent book *Religion and Political Culture in Kano.*[259]

As a spiritual guide in Sufism (*taṣawwuf*), Shaykh Ibrāhīm wrote many books explaining Sufism and the possibility of spiritual perfection in the modern age. Perhaps the most famous and widely read is the *Kāshif al-ilbās*, or "The Removal of Confusion."[260] Written in Arabic (as with his other writings), it explains the real meaning of Sufism. In it, the Shaykh states that *taṣawwuf* possesses a definition, subject matter, name, compilers, sources, laws, problems, benefits, attributes, and results. Everyone who takes up its study should be familiar with these ten points. According to the Shaykh, *taṣawwuf* is adopting every worthy form of behavior and eschewing every unworthy form of action. It is to adopt, in fact, the character of the Qur'ān and Sunnah. One must give himself entirely over to Allāh, the Exalted, in whatever He wills, just as He wills. A certain poet quoted in the *Kāshif* once said, "Sufism is not to wear woolen garments or affect worn out clothing. It is good behavior and good manners (*adab*)." Another said, "Sufism is

259 John Paden, *Religion and Political Culture in Kano* (Berkeley: University of California Press, 1973).

260 For a full translation of this work, see Ibrāhīm Niasse, *The Removal of Confusion Concerning the Flood of the Saintly Seal Aḥmad al-Tijānī* (trans. Zachary Wright, Muhtar Holland, ʿAbd-Allāhi el-Okene, Louisville, Kentucky: Fons Vitae, 2010).

not to wear a woolen coat and patch it, nor to weep when the singer sings. It is not to cry out, nor to dance and make merry. It is not to feign fainting as if one is mad. Rather, Sufism is being pure without defilement and following the truth of Qur᾿ān and the religion."

Shaykh Ibrāhīm was the best example of the description, "The Sufi is the son of his hour (*ibn waqtihi*)." He will respond to the needs of the time and deal with the requirements of every moment. The Muslim who is greatest in understanding is he who submits to the rule of his hour. That is, he gives everything to the position it requires in action and speech. He is a person moving with time in a circle. He does not attempt to stop time, become stagnant in it, or regress in it. His effort is aimed at continually moving forward. In the season of Ramadan, he reads Qur᾿ān and Ḥadīth and presents their explanations. In the season of *Ḥājj*, he expounds the virtues of the Muslim pilgrimage. At the time of *Mawlid*, he recounts the Prophet's biography. All of this behavior characterized the Sufism of Shaykh Ibrāhīm. It was based on action and practice – traveling all over the Muslim world, giving speeches and writing pamphlets. In every endeavor, his goal was to direct Muslims to the right path (*al-ṣirāṭ al-mustaqīm*). Sickness did not bother him unless it halted his activity in spreading Islam. Indeed, his *taṣawwuf* was not characterized by heedlessness and neglect (*ghafla*). It was based on real Islam, which includes mastering the self (*nafs*) and ruling over it with Qur᾿ān and Sunnah. His affiliation with Sufism likewise did not preclude his being a productive member of the society, and he engaged in farming and other beneficial activities. His followers emulated him by working on farms, in universities, in government, industry, and parliament.

Among his followers, Shaykh Ibrāhīm encouraged a love of both knowledge and truth. Throughout his life, his viewpoints on education and literacy were remarkably forward-looking. Literacy is generally a priority among members of the Ṭarīqa and the Tijāniyya is known for its scholars. It is called the "Ṭarīqa of the ʿulamāʾ" and encourages scholarship for everyone. As a result, one finds many schools teaching Arabic, Qurʾān, and religious studies, as well as the natural sciences and mathematics.

The Shaykh advocated the education of both men and women. The "Reformed Tijaniyya" opened many doors for women in Africa.[261] The teaching of women is an obligation (*farḍ*) among Muslims, such that if their teaching is neglected the entire Muslim community (*umma*) is at fault. Hence, one finds many women among the Shaykh's followers who have become scholars and *muqaddams* in their own right: women well versed in Arabic who teach, lecture, and write books. In fact, many women in the community have memorized the entire Qurʾān and many Ḥadīths. And even women who cannot read or write know the laws of Sharīʿa and early Islamic history, due to the Shaykh's tireless efforts to explain the religion in the local Wolof language. With reference to women, the Shaykh said in a speech, "Women should compete with men in knowledge."

The Shaykh encouraged those following him to learn Arabic and Islam well in order to stand as a bulwark against false doctrines. By the same token, his mind was not closed to learning other languages besides Arabic. He said, "Had I known more languages, I could have reached more people. Whoever travels and does not know Arabic and English, or Arabic and French might well have stayed at home because he will have gained nothing."

Many of the Shaykh's sons have received extensive education in Egypt, Qatar, Morocco, Libya, and London. Besides Islamic studies, they are well educated in many fields – such

---

261 For more on this subject, see Alaine Hutson, "The Development of Women's Authority in the Kano Tijaniyya, 1894-1963," in *Africa Today* (1999).

as Economics, Diplomacy, Political Science, Agriculture, and Education.

In his speech for the *Mawlid*, 1386 A.H (1966), the Shaykh addressed Muslim youth and said:

> *For the youth, I thank you all for your papers. And I am here to tell you to go ahead and be in the vanguard of things. Surely the future of every nation is based on its youth. But not upon all of them, not upon every individual, but only on the intellectual ones: the educated ones with good character, good manners, and zeal for knowledge. As for the youth lacking education and good character, they are like seeds unfertilized. So make every effort to seek out and acquire more knowledge, not only Islamic knowledge, not only mathematics and its branches, but also be part of and cooperate with those whose zeal is to discover the unknown and unseen things of this world.*

Shaykh Ibrāhīm played a major role in the Muslim world. He was a member of many organizations: the Muslim World League (*Rābiṭat al-ʿĀlam al-Islāmī*) based in Mecca; the Muslim World Congress (*Muʾtamar ʿĀlam al-Islām*) based in Karachi, Pakistan; and the Islamic Research Assembly (*Majmaʿ al-Buḥūth al-Islāmiyya*) and the High Council of Islamic Affairs (*Majlis al-ʿAlā li al-Shuʾūn al-Islāmiyya*), both of which are based in Egypt. In all of these organizations he was highly regarded especially for his religious writings, which include many articles, poems, and some forty-nine books all in Arabic.

Yet it was not only religious organizations that held Shaykh Ibrāhīm in esteem. Many governments also honored him. Among his many awards for excellence are the Medallion of the Throne from Morocco, the Medallion of the Republic of Tunisia, the Medallion of Nigeria, the Legion of Honor in France, and the Medal of Merit of the Society of Ancient Warriors also from France. He received several medals from the government of Senegal among the highest was the Grand Croix. He also received an honorary doctorate from Libya.

Throughout his life Shaykh Ibrāhīm's character was based on the Qur'ān and the Sunnah of the Prophet. Muslim leaders close to him testified to this and praised him for it. For example, a letter of Shaykh Muḥammad alḤāfiẓ alTijānī, the Egyptian who was known as the first man of Ḥadīth in his age, opens:

> *Praise belongs to Allāh, for Allāh has blessed us by binding in love this humble servant Muḥammad al-Ḥāfiẓ al-Tijānī and the Ḥujja, the cornerstone of the religion, the sea of confidence, the believer in Allāh, my brother and the brother of my spirit, my master Abī Isḥāq, Shaykh Ibrāhīm ....*

In his greeting, it is important to note that Shaykh al-Ḥāfiẓ uses the word *Ḥujja* – Arabic for "the proof" – as a form of address. The scholars of Ḥadīth rank the scholars who work in this field, and each rank has a specific name. For example, the "*muḥaddith*" is the narrator of Ḥadīth who reads traditions based upon narration and report. The "*ḥāfiẓ*" has memorized one hundred thousand Ḥadīth along with their explanation. But the "*ḥujja*" has memorized three hundred thousand Ḥadīths with their explanations and chains of transmission.

In a letter dated 1381/1962 from the Secretary General of the World Muslim League in Mecca, Shaykh Muḥammad Suruj alSabban, Shaykh Ibrāhīm is addressed as follows:

> *To the owner of virtue, member of the Islamic Conference, wellrespected brother, Shaykh Ibrāhīm Niasse, Assalamu Alaikum. Peace be upon you, and the mercy of Allāh, and His Blessing be upon you. The pioneers have left the Hijaz, with the propagators of the religion. They also left with the understanding (fiqh) of the Hijaz, and now it remains in you Shaykh Ibrāhīm. They have*

also left with the style of reading Qur'ān with which the people of Hijaz used to recite, and you have remained reading the word of Allāh with the same style of the Hijaz, the style of Nafi Mawla Abī Nu'aym. Indeed, you are among the real people of Medina in both Fiqh and Qur'ān. These are the proofs of your steadfastness, and this is not pride for me but for you, by Him. You have steadfastly believed, protected, and spread the religion victoriously.

Shaykh Ibrāhīm was indeed a very hardworking man throughout his life. I saw him in the hospital toward the end of his life, when his doctor had repeatedly tried to induce him to sleep with powerful medications. It was almost in vain. The longest period he slept was four hours. Of this the Shaykh said, "Since I reached the age of thirty, I have never slept more than two hours a day."

In these passages we have focused primarily on the character and virtues of this distinguished leader of modern times, Shaykh Ibrāhīm Niasse. Much remains to be said, particularly about his role in the contemporary politics of Senegal and the Muslim world. But this must wait for another occasion.

Important works of Shaykh Ibrāhim Nīasse

The following list includes all of the Arabic sources translated here. But it is not a comprehensive list of the Shaykh's writings. For such a list, see the entry on Ibrāhīm Niasse by Ousmane Kane and Rüdiger Seesemann in John Hunwick (ed) The Arabic Literature of Africa, volume 4: The Writings of Western Sudanic Africa (Leiden: Brill, 2003). The following list is arranged roughly by the length of the text.

* * *

Fī riyāḍ al-tafsīr li l-Qur'ān al-karīm. 6 vols Tunis: al-Yamāna, 2010.

Jawāhir al-rasā'il wa yaliya ziyāda al-jawāhir al-hāwī ba'ḍ 'ulūm wasīla al-wasā'il. 3 vols (Nigeria): Aḥmad Abī al-Fatḥ, unknown date.

Kāshif al-ilbās 'an fayḍa al-khatm Abī al-'Abbās. Cairo: al-Sharika al-dawliyya, 2001.

Sa'āda al-anām bi aqwāl Shaykh al-Islām. Cairo: al-sharika al-dawliyya li-l-ṭibā'a, 2006.

*Itḥā*f al-sāmi' *wa l-rāwī bi ba'ḍ ajwiba al-Shaykh wa l-fatāwī*. Cairo: al-sharika al-dawliyya li-l-ṭibā'a, 2012.

Dawāwīn al-sitt. Dakar: Muḥammad Ma'mun Niasse, 1988.

Jāmi' al-jawāmi' al-dawāwīn. Dakar: Muḥammad Ma'mun Niasse, 1988.

Al-Budūr al-suṭa' sharḥ al-murhafāt al-quṭa'. Egypt: al-Nahār, 2007.

Raf' al-malām 'amman rafa'a wa qabaḍa iqtidā'an bi sayyid al-anām. Cairo: al-Mashhad al-Husayni, unknown date.

Kanz al-maṣūn. Rabat: Shaykh Tijānī Cissé, 2007.

Majmū' riḥlāt al-shaykh Ibrāhīm. Dakar: Muḥammad Ma'mūn Niasse, 1988.

*Tabṣīrat al-anām fī ann al-'ilm huwa al-im*ām. Kaolack, Senegal: Maktabat al-Nahḍa, 2006.

"Al-Sirr al-akbar wa l-kabrīt al-aḥmar." MS in Northwestern Library, Falke Collection, 30, 1933.

Secondary Sources in European Languages

Brigaglia, Andrea. "The Fayda Tijaniyya of Ibrāhīm Nyass: Genesis and Implications of a Sufi Doctrine." *Islam et sociétés au sud du Sahara* 14-15 (2001): 41-56.

Cissé, Ḥasan b. ʿAlī. *Shaykh Ibrahim Niasse: Revivalist of the Sunnah*. New York: Tariqa Tijaniyya of New York Publications, 1984.

Cissé, Ḥasan b. ʿAlī. *The Spirit of Good Morals by Shaykh al-Islam Ibrahim Niasse, Translation and Commentary*. Detroit, MI: African American Islamic Institute, 2001.

Cissé, al-Tijānī b. ʿAlī. *Knowing Allah, Living Islam*. Singapore: Light of Eminence, 2014.

Gray, Christopher. "The Rise of the Niassene Tijaniyya, 1875 to the Present." In *Islam et Islamismes au Sud du Sahara*, edited by Ousmane Kane and Jean-Louis Triaud, 59-82. Paris: Karthala, 1998.

Hill, Joseph. "Divine Knowledge and Islamic Authority: Religious Specialization among Disciples of Baay Ñas." PhD dissertation. Yale University, 2007.

Hiskett, Mervyn, "The Community of Grace and Its Opponents, the Rejecters: A Debate about Theology and Mysticism in Muslim West Africa with Special Reference to its Hausa Expression." *African Language Studies* 17 (1980): 99-140.

Kane, Ousmane. "Shaikh al-Islam al-Hajj Ibrahim Niasse." In *Le Temps des Marabouts: Itinéraires et Stratégies Islamiques en Afrique Occidentale Française v. 1880-1960*, edited by David Robinson and Jean-Louis Triaud, 299-316. Paris: Karthala, 1997.

Mohammed, Ahmed Rufai. "The Influence of the Niass Tijaniyya in the Niger-Benue Confluence Area of Niger." In *Muslim Identity and Social Change in Sub-Saharan Africa*, edited by Louis Brenner. Bloomington: Indiana University Press, 1993.

Niasse, Mouhamadou Mahdy. *Baye Niass: Le Défenseur de l'Islam*. Montreal: Alioune Thiam, 1997.

Seesemann, Rüdiger. *The Divine Flood: Ibrāhīm Niasse and the Roots of a Twentieth-Century Sufi Revival*. New York: Oxford University Press, 2011.

Thiam, Mbaye. *Cheikh el Islam el Hadji Ibrahima Niasse: Imam de la Faydatou al Tidiania*. Dakar, 2013.

Wright, Zachary. *Living Knowledge in West African Islam: the Sufi Community of Ibrāhīm Niasse*. Leiden, Netherlands: Brill, 2015.

CPSIA information can be obtained
at www.ICGtesting.com
Printed in the USA
BVHW041645031019
560144BV00007B/128/P

9 780991 381395